I Wor

Badge

By

DENNIS L. SHELTON

ABOUT THE AUTHOR

I majored in Sociology at Southern Illinois University and had a minor in English.

I then went into the military and spent two years. Once out of the military, I put my application in at the Jackson County Sheriff's Department, and after three months, I got the job. I started there in October of 1972.

After putting thirty years in at the Sheriff's Department, I retired for a few years, then worked for the Southern Illinois Airport Police. I left there as the Police Chief after fifteen years.

DEDICATION

I dedicate this book to my good friend and co-worker, R.D. Youngberg (Dave Youngberg). I have known Dave for almost forty-five years and have enjoyed working with him for over twenty-five years. Dave always had my back, on duty and off. I miss you very much, my brother.

RIP

TABLE OF CONTENTS

IN THE BEGINNING

In high school, I decided then that I wanted to go into law enforcement. After high school, I went to college, and after college, I got drafted into the military during Viet Nam. I spent two years in the military, and once out, I applied at the Jackson County Sheriff's Department for a job as a Deputy Sheriff. I got hired three months later and went to work there in October of 1972.

Once hired at the Sheriff's Department, it was policy then that one would spend time working the jail as a jail officer as a prerequisite for working the road as a Deputy. I worked in the jail for approximately three months, thinking I would be assigned to the road. However, the Sheriff at the time stated once working the jail, he wanted new hires to work the radio after working in the jail. The Sheriff advised he wanted each new hire to know how to work both. I spent a couple of months working the radio as a dispatcher, then was assigned to the road as a road Deputy.

When assigned to the road, it was a policy that one would ride with a veteran Officer until he thought you were ready to be on your own on the road. After riding for approximately a month, I was assigned a road position as Deputy Sheriff. A short time later, I went to the Police Training Institute in Champaign, Illinois, which the State of Illinois mandates. After graduating from the Police Training Institute, I returned to work as a Deputy Sheriff.

I soon learned that one can't always go by the book when dealing with people - that basically is a learned thing. I had an instructor at the Police Training Institute, and he stated he was teaching a class (mainly veteran Officers) and telling the class how to deal with a rowdy person in a bar and get them out of the bar without any trouble. The instructor stated that one of the Officers in the class spoke up and asked him if he had ever been on the road as an Officer. The instructor said, "No, he had not."

The Officer told him to come out and ride with him some night, put his theory into practice, and see if it worked. The Officer told the instructor, "I guarantee your theory will not work." The instructor stated he took the Officer up on his offer. When riding, the instructor stated they received a call of a rowdy patron in a bar that the establishment wanted to be removed. The Officer told the instructor to handle this call, and he would be the backup. The instructor stated they went in, and he started talking to the rowdy patron the way he said they should be talked to in class, and the instructor stated he got kicked right in the groin. He never taught his theory after that. Experience is the best teacher...

Upon going to work on the road, I soon learned that camaraderie was a big factor in law enforcement. The other Officers working with you soon became like family to you and very good friends. Some friends I once had before going into law enforcement seemed to shy away from me now that I was a Police Officer.

Apparently, they didn't feel comfortable about hanging out with Law Enforcement. These friends had never been in trouble with the law before, and it was hard for me to understand. But I remembered what was said at the Police Training Institute, and they said some friends would shy away from you when you become a "cop." How true.... but a shame.

When I was assigned to the road as a Road Deputy, the Sheriff's Department was just implementing patrol. At that time, if something occurred, it was customary that the Illinois State Police would handle it. For example, if there was a bar fight, the Illinois State Police would be called, and it may take them a while to get there. The Trooper assigned may be in Mt. Vernon when he got the call. The people in the fight all new the Illinois State Police would be called, and they were used to the Police not getting there very fast. So, when we started patrolling, it surprised everyone when we started arriving on the scene and making arrests. After a while, fights started calming down because the people involved knew someone was going to jail.

Chapter 1

Don't Assume Suicide

I soon learned that being a road Deputy, one had to have common sense and a "gift to gab." You wouldn't make it as a road deputy if you didn't have both factors.

During the daytime, the daytime patrol would just patrol the county and patrol pretty much wherever they wanted to go. Jackson County is approximately 635 square miles, and that's a lot of area to cover. During night patrol, the county was divided into four squares at night. The squares were classified as Zone 1, Zone 2, Zone 3, and Zone 4. Then the Supervisor would be the Rove car, in that if one of the zone cars received a call that needed a backup Officer, the Rove car would go to the call also. The Supervisor assigned zones. I always wanted Zone 1 or Zone 2. Zone 1 was everything east of South Rt #127, south of Carbondale to the eastern Jackson County line. Zone 2 was everything east of North Rt #127, north of Carbondale to the eastern Jackson County line. I liked these two zones because these were the zones most of the calls came into. However, Officers usually rotated zones each night.

When I first got onto the road, I was working the road on the day shift. Deputy Bob Scott and I worked together on this shift except on our days off. I remember Deputy Scott was off, and I was working the road by myself during the day. The first call I ever received was a possible suicide call. Once receiving a call, it goes through your mind on the way to the call how you will proceed once you get there.

A female had called the Sheriff's Department and stated she lived in a trailer just south of McGuire's Orchard. She stated that she and her husband had gotten into an argument, and he threw her out of the trailer. She stated as she was walking up to the house by the trailer, she heard a gun go off inside the trailer, and she assumed her husband had shot himself.

I arrived a short time later by myself with no backup Officer. Upon arriving, I spoke briefly with the complainant, and she informed me of what the dispatcher had previously stated. I asked if she had been battered, and she stated she had been. I asked if she wanted to sign a complaint, and she said she did. I then let her sign an NTA form for Battery. It was the law then that a complaint had to be signed in a battery case for an arrest to be made. I got the complaint signed before talking to her husband to cover myself if any force had to be used to arrest him.

I walked up to the trailer door and knocked. I heard no one inside, and I checked to see if the door was unlocked, which it was. Once opening the door, I yelled, "Sheriff's Department, anyone here?" I could see the living room and kitchen area, and that was all I had a visual of. I assumed a closed sliding door in the kitchen went back to the bedrooms.

Standing outside the trailer's entrance door, I aimed my service weapon at this sliding door and yelled, "Sheriff's Department, anyone in the back?" I yelled this twice and then heard what appeared to be a shotgun shell being loaded into a shotgun. I yelled that I had my service weapon aimed at the door, and whoever was back there to come out with their hands up; if not, I would shoot. After a few seconds, I heard a male subject yell that he was back there, and I ordered him to come out with his hands up, to which he complied. I then placed the subject under arrest for battery and placed him in the back seat of my squad. The shotgun was then confiscated for evidence. While en route to the jail, I asked the subject if he had intentions of shooting it out with me, and he refused to answer my question.

This is where common sense comes in. On a call like this, one does not assume to have a body lying inside just because someone heard a shot go off. The suspect informed me that he had fired the shotgun from the bathroom window to make his wife think he had shot himself. I sincerely believe if I had walked into that trailer under the assumption of an apparent suicide, I would have been shot.

CHAPTER 2

ASSIST MURPHYSBORO P.D. WITH SUICIDE

One warm summer night, I was working the midnight shift, and I think it was around 10:00 PM that evening I heard Murphysboro Police receive a call of a large fire on North 7th street. MPD asked for our assistance, and I then proceeded to the location. I hadn't been there except for a few minutes, and Sgt. Glodo asked me if I would assist him with a possible suicide off South 20th Street.

While en route, I heard the Murphysboro dispatcher advise us the location was on south 20th Street, the alley just south of Jackson Street. Dispatcher advised that the caller had called in and stated that she and her husband had had an argument, and he stated he was going out to the garage and shooting himself. The caller said she heard a shot go off once her husband got to the garage.

We then arrived in the area and turned into the alley just south of Jackson Street. Sgt. Glodo advised me via radio to help him check the garages as we drove by them, for he wasn't sure which garage it would be. A few seconds later, I heard Sgt. Glodo advised me over the radio, "Look out." My left hand was on the squad car's spotlight, and I saw a male figure standing inside a garage to my right. I moved the spotlight to shine in the garage, and when I moved the spotlight to illuminate the inside, somehow, I shied the light right in the eyes of the suspect. He had a handgun in his hand, and I saw him turn his head about ten degrees to his right due to the spotlight shining in his eyes. At the same time, he fired a round off at me, for I could see the muzzle blast go off in my

4

direction. I had not been able to exit the squad yet. I do not know how the round fired missed me or missed hitting my squad car, for it appeared to be pointing right at me. No doubt, God was watching over me that night.

Sgt. Glodo nor I could not see the subject inside the garage now, and Sgt. Glodo radioed dispatch for more units to come to the scene. Once the other units were there, we approached the garage since we couldn't get any response from the subject inside. We located the subject behind a parked car in the garage. He was on his knees and had shot himself in the head with the handgun. Neither Sgt. Glodo nor I heard the fatal shot go off.

Upon talking to the suspect's wife, we learned he had told her he was going to commit suicide, but he was going to take a cop with him before shooting himself. She further stated that he had gone to the funeral home and had made his funeral arrangements a few days earlier. The wife had not told the Murphysboro Police dispatcher this when she called in the report.

The victim's wife could have very well gotten me or Sgt. Glodo killed for failing to report all the information at the time.

Chapter 3

DEPUTY NICHOLS WITH FAULTY SHOTGUN

When I started working at the Sheriff's Department, the Sheriff's Office was at the south end of the Court House. Across the street on Chestnut Street was a bar that the black subjects drank and congregated in front of on Friday and Saturday nights.

I came to work one Friday night and went inside the Sheriff's Office, and met up with the other Deputies coming on duty. After a brief shift meeting and getting zones assigned, we went to a closet where the shotguns and other weapons were stored, and each Deputy checked a shotgun out. We had one shotgun that would discharge automatically once jacking a round in the chamber. This weapon was supposed to be marked and sent off for repair. Apparently not...

Deputy Dave Nichols, unfortunately, obtained this malfunctioning weapon and was loading it while walking out of the Sheriff's Office. Once out of the entrance door to the courthouse, Deputy Nichols stopped and jacked a round in the chamber, and the shotgun went off. As previously stated, black male and female subjects would congregate across the street from our office at this bar. When the shotgun was discharged, people ran in all directions as fast as they could. I never saw a sole around that bar the rest of the night after this incident.

CHAPTER 4

TOUGH TIME FOR ME

A Police Officer's life is different than that of an ordinary citizen. We work crazy hours, rotate to different shifts, and must go to court after maybe working all night. And once out of court, we may have a couple of hours before going on our next shift. It was hard on my marriage, but it could have been because I loved my job so much.

In 1982, I got divorced and moved out of my house. Murphysboro Police Officer Don Fenton told me he had an apartment in the basement of his mother's house he had been staying at, and he would move out and let me rent it cheap if I wanted it. I immediately took it, for I had nowhere else to go.

I moved in and didn't have much, but I had what I needed. I remember my budget now was 69 cents a day, which was tough after living my previous lifestyle. I remember Farm Fresh in Murphysboro was a few blocks from my apartment. They sold TV dinners there, and they were 69 cents each. So, I ate a tv dinner every day. When I went to work, I would go to the kitchen to see if the cook had anything left over from fixing the jail meals. Sometimes she did; other times, she didn't. I'd leave on patrol and drive by Hardees or McDonalds, and when looking over, I remember thinking to myself, I wished I had just enough money for a hamburger.

It was sort of a tradition that two or three of us on a shift would meet at Denny's Restaurant in Carbondale sometime during the shift. Sometimes while taking a break, if a State Trooper were in the area, he would also pull in and join us. I remember everyone ordering things to eat, and I'm sitting there starving. A couple of the guys would look at me and say, "Aren't you going to eat?" I told them I wasn't hungry because I had brought my lunch. I'd sit there and drink water, or one of the guys would put my coffee on his tab. I wasn't about to tell them my financial situation, that I couldn't even afford a cup of coffee.

I remember going to St. Joseph Hospital one evening on a call, and one of the nurses there told me, "You look like you've lost a lot of weight Denny." I told her I was on a diet...

When I started getting a little better financially, I moved out of Don Fenton's apartment so he could have it back and moved into an apartment of my own. I didn't have a table or furniture in the apartment, not even a bed. I remember Dennis Inman, who used to own the Dumoroc tavern; he figured out what was happening and called me up to his bar one night while I was working, wanting to talk to me. Dennis asked me if I needed a table or any furniture, and I told him I could use a table to eat on. He took me to the back of the bar, a large room full of furniture, and he told me to take what I needed free of charge. I will always be grateful for his generosity.

The general public doesn't think of a Police Officer as having a personal life. All they see is a uniform and a badge. They never know what an Officer might be going through off duty. Me, I made it fine. It was tough, but I overcame it thanks to God's will and help.

CHAPTER 5

I DISOBEYED THE SHERIFF

Not too long after I started at the Sheriff's Department, I was sent to a domestic call in Dowell. Upon arrival, I learned that no battery had been committed, the married couple was just arguing, and we were called by either the husband or the wife, I can't remember. I arrived a short time later, and after a discussion, I asked the male subject if there was anywhere I could take him until he and his wife cooled down. He said no, he wasn't leaving.

In Dowell at the time, there was nothing open in that town this time of the evening except two bars in town. I told the male subject, why don't you let me take you to one of the bars here in town and have a coke or coffee until things die down? He finally consented, and his wife was glad to see him leave.

The next day I came to work at 3:00 PM, working the evening shift. When I walked into the Sheriff's Office, the dispatcher stopped me and told me the Sheriff was waiting to see me and for me to go upstairs to his quarters. The Sheriff during this time lived on the third floor of the courthouse where the jail is. I'm not going to mention this Sheriff by name.

Once upstairs, the Sheriff started jumping over me about the domestic call I handled in Dowell the day before. He told me I would go to Dowell, contact the lady of the husband I took to the bar, and apologize. I said, "For what?" The Sheriff stated the lady had called in, and I told her husband I would take him to the bar, and he could sit there and get drunk. Sheriff stated, "You took him to VanZandt's bar and dropped him off." I told the Sheriff that was

9

not what happened, and he wouldn't let me explain. He told me to leave right now and apologize to the lady. I told the Sheriff, "I am not going up there. I am not going to apologize for something I didn't say." The Sheriff ordered me to go up there, and I told him, "I will not." I told him again; I wouldn't apologize for something I didn't say. I turned around and walked off, and left. I figured my law enforcement days were done now.

However, that was the last I ever heard about it. The next time I saw the Sheriff, he was as cordial and friendly as he could be and never brought the subject of that domestic up again.

When I became Sgt. somewhere around the mid-1980s, if I had a complaint about a Deputy, I would first get his side of the story before deciding.

This Sheriff never asked me my side of the story.

CHAPTER 6

ENCOUNTER WITH A JUDGE

One night the Desoto Officer, Vince Burns, brought in a subject for Driving While Under the Influence. During this period, when a person was arrested for DUI, they had 90 minutes to decide if they wanted to take the breathalyzer test once they were read the DUI warning.

It was a slow night, and I entered the Sheriff's Office to see if I could assist Officer Burns. Burns informed me the subject stated he was going to wait his 90 minutes before he decided on whether he was going to take the breathalyzer or not. Officer Burns informed me that the subject had called his attorney and was waiting for him. I will not mention the attorney's name.

In a short while, the attorney walked in, and right off the get-go, the attorney started telling Officer Burns what he would do and not do. The attorney kept getting irate by the minute for no reason. He never even talked to his client. After about five minutes of listening to this attorney rant and rave, I asked him if he had any advice for his client. He stated yes, he told his client not to take the test. The attorney then started yelling at me and Officer Burns.

I then told the attorney to get out of my Office; he was no longer needed here, and for him to leave. If he didn't leave, he would be arrested for obstructing. After a few words, the attorney left. He later became a Judge in Jackson County, and he and I got along great after that. Nothing was ever brought up between him and me over that incident.

CHAPTER 7

MARIE AZEVEDO MURDER

This is one of the most notorious murders in Jackson County, at least while I was working there.

On March 25, 1981, Marie Azevedo was employed by SIU, and before going to work, she dropped her kids off at school at the babysitter. She never made it to work. On April 1st, her car was found in a wooded area on the NE side of Carbondale. Inside was Mrs. Azevedo; she had been shot numerous times from both sides of the car. She had been divorced from her husband, Dr. Allan Azevedo, who was a dentist in Murphysboro. She and her husband had been going through a bitter divorce, and upon the divorce being final, she was awarded custody of the four children. Both she and her husband had been fighting for custody.

Allan Azevedo became the chief suspect in the case, and three days after his wife's body had been found, he consented to a polygraph in which he passed. Even though he passed the polygraph, he remained the chief suspect in his wife's murder.

Dr. Azevedo's office was in Murphysboro, however, he contracted work with Menard Prison, in that he would go there and treat inmates. It was believed there that he tried to contract his wife's murder while at the prison. The El Rukins was one of the most notorious street gangs out of Chicago in which they dealt drugs and weapons.

Dr. Azevedo apparently made a deal with the El Rukins to murder his wife. He gave them a down payment but failed to pay them what he owed on the balance. The El Rukins then started threatening Azevedo and being scared he turned to the Police to help him. Azevedo's phone was now tapped, and from the Police listening to the conversations between the El Rukins and Azevedo, they thought they had enough evidence to charge him. In March 1985, Azevedo was charged with trying to hire someone to kill his wife.

When the case went to trial, some of the El Rukins were brought to Murphysboro for the trial. The whole case basically revolved around the El Rukins members' testimony. However, Judge Richman dismissed the charges against Azevedo. He stated that portions of the El Rukins testimony were inadmissible. In July 29, 1985, Judge Richman gave a direct verdict of not guilty. Azevedo was now a free man.

In late September 1985, I received a call to go to Azevedo's residence which was located east of Murphysboro on Old Rt #13, on apparent suspicious activity. Upon arrival, I found no vehicle at the residence, and being the house was unlocked, I checked inside the residence and found no one. Not too long after that, Dr. Azevedo's body was found in his car with him being shot twice in the chest. Approximately two weeks later, Azevedo's son Andrew, age 15, confessed to shooting his father.

Andrew confessed to shooting his father while he was sleeping, and Andrew then called a friend of his to come and help load his dad's body in the car. Andrew was tried as a juvenile, and was sentenced by Judge Richman to DOC, Harrisburg juvenile facility, until age 21. No one was ever brought to justice for the murder of Marie Azevedo. She was buried at Tower Grove Cemetery NW of Murphysboro. On her tombstone it reads only, "Marie Azevedo 1944 to 1981."

CHAPTER 8

THE RAILROAD KILLER

Angel Maturino Resendiz

In June of 1999, Jackson County had a serial killer come through its county. Angel Resendiz was a Mexican immigrant, who traveled the rails on freight trains. He hopped off a freight train in Gorham, Il, and was sleeping in a wooded area behind the residence belonging to 80 yr old George Morber. Morber lived next to the railroad tracks, and Resendiz stayed close to the tracks.

Resendiz saw Morber leaving in his truck, and Resendiz then climbed through the window of Morber's house. Morber had just driven down to the end of his driveway to get the newspaper and came right back. He was startled to find someone inside his residence when he was just gone for a couple of minutes. Resendiz then tied Morber up with a cord to a chair, and Resendiz then shot Morber in the head once killing him with his own shotgun. A few minutes later, Morber's daughter Carolyn age 51, arrived to clean her dad's house. Once inside the residence, Resendiz beat her with the butt end of the shotgun he had used on her father. He hit her so many times and so hard, the shotgun split into.

Resendez then spent quite a bit of time inside Morber's home after he murdered the two. He sat and read the paper and helped himself to Morber's food. When leaving, he took George Morber's truck, and the truck was found approximately 70 miles away.

The murder was making everyone nervous in Jackson County. I have railroad tracks behind my house. Several days I would take my service weapon, go and sit on the deck of my pool watching the railroad tracks. I would pray that the killer would come up to me. Obviously, he never did. Resendez killed fifteen people before he was ever caught, and he was called the "Railroad Killer.

Resendez was never charged with the murder of the Morber's since he was in custody in Texas, but he confessed to killing them. On June 27, 2006, Resendez was executed in Texas by lethal injection.

CHAPTER 9

WARRANT SERVICE

I came to work one day and learned that we had an arrest warrant for Jeff Com (will not use his real name). Com was a well-known troublemaker in Jackson County, and had a extensive criminal past. We were always having warrants on him or getting a complaint on him for something he had done to someone else.

Deputy Dave Youngberg and I went to Ava to execute the warrant. We knew he had been staying in Ava and was allegedly staying with Phillip Bramlett's sister. Upon arrival at the scene, a white female subject came to the door, and I informed her that we had an arrest warrant for Jeff Com, and asked if he was there. Female informed us he was not, for she had not seen him. I then stated, "you don't mind if we search the residence then?" Female invited us in, and Deputy Youngberg and I started search the residence.

We searched the residence twice and could not find Com inside the residence. I informed Deputy Youngberg, that Com had to be in the residence, I just had a feeling. I told Youngberg we needed to search one more time for the subject. Deputy Youngberg agreed with me, and we began to search again.

Deputy Youngberg went into one of the bedrooms that we had previously searched and looked in the closet again. This time Youngberg saw feet on the floor of the closet behind some clothes hanging up. I heard Youngberg inform Com to come out of the closet at a loud tone. I immediately went to this bedroom, and entered when Com was coming out of the closet. He came out in an irate manner, telling us we would have to both fight him for he was not going to be arrested. Com stated he would kick both of our ass's. About that time, I pulled my pepper spray out, and hosed him down. I used approximately half a can of pepper spray in his face. Com then fell to the floor like he was knocked out. He was then immediately handcuffed and transported to the Jackson County Jail.

When booked in, he was told to take a shower, which he complied. Once out of the shower, Com walked up to the desk I was sitting at doing paperwork, and stated, "that pepper spray is wicked man." I looked up at Com, and his face was completely swollen and red. It looked as though 50 wasps had gotten a hold of him. I had never seen pepper spray affect anyone like this. I just looked up and Com and told him, "You will never learn Jeff," and went back to my paperwork.

Surprisingly, Com was cooperative with the jail staff, and making jokes about the effect of pepper spray on his face. He acted proud of it, like it was a war wound or something.

Obviously, that was not the last time we dealt wit the subject.

CHAPTER 10

TEACHING DEPUTY WILSON TO REVIEW HIS RE-PORTS

Sometimes, being a Police Officer has its lighter moments. Police Officers often joke around with each other and play jokes on one another and it's just a way of relieving stress. For example.... On Sunday nights, I tried, if we were not busy to go in the Office, sit down at the computer in the report writing room, and catch up on reports. Upon going into the Office, Deputy Mark Wilson was writing reports also.

We talked briefly, and I then sat down and started doing my reports. After about thirty minutes, Deputy Wilson made the statement, "Well, I'm done. I'm going to go up in the dispatch room for a while." He then left to go to the dispatch office, and I moved over to look at his report when he left. He had been writing a sexual molestation report on a young girl. I thought to myself, "I can have a field day with this."

In a report the abbreviation for Investigating Officer is IO, or RO for Reporting Officer. Wilson in this report was using the IO in his report. There was a part of the report where Wilson had been talking about a little girl being on a swing set at her school. I then put in the report, "IO saw the little girl, and I then hid behind a tree that was close by. I then started watching her hoping to get a glimpse of her panties, and at the same time was fondling myself." I went through his report, and made several insertions of this nature, and then moved back over to start back doing my reports.

A short time later, Deputy Wilson came back into the report writing room, and started joking around with me. A few minutes later, Wilson said he was going to print his report out and turn it in and get back on patrol. Wilson then started to hit the print button, and I asked him, "don't you proofread your reports?" Jokingly he said, "I never do, and hit the print button." I then started laughing and told him I think he had better proofread this report. Wilson looked at me sort of funny and sat down and started going through the report. When he came upon the insertions I had made in the report, I can't repeat what he said to me. Both of us started laughing and got a good laugh out of the incident. To this day, he and I still talk about this incident and have a good laugh.

To the public, this may seem unprofessional, childish, and immature. However, a Police officer's job is different than any other job there is. We have our ways of relieving stress and coping with the day-to-day job around each other. Police Officers are very close to each other. We can do things like this, and no one gets mad over it. Why? Because we all do it to relieve stress and cope with the job, for we are all brothers doing the same job. Five minutes after a joke is pulled, we may be saving each other's life on the street. Every day on the job is different, one never knows what will happen. Just another reason cops hang out with cops.

Chapter 11

MICHAEL MILEY MURDER

Subject Michael Miley had been reported missing by his father, and on April 9th, 1988, his vehicle was found abandoned south of Carbondale. The vehicle was partially burned, and in the trunk of the car was a body which had been decapitated. The body was later identified as Michael Miley.

Michael Miley

Miley worked at a restaurant in Carbondale and associated with the gay community. In the late 1980's, there was a nearby lake known as Crab Orchard Lake, that the gays all met up and congregated at. Several hate crimes were being committed at this time towards the gays at the lake. Michael had a twin brother by the name of Mark, and he happened to have his car beat in with a baseball bat. Rumor was that the suspect was Richard Nitz who lived in Carbondale, who had an extensive criminal history. No one could prove it was Nitz doing the vandalism to the cars, however.

On the night Miley was murdered, subject by the name of Betty Boyer told the Police she looked out her window after hearing a commotion and saw Richard Nitz beating Michael Miley in the head with a baseball bat. Miley was not moving, and she stated she saw Richard Nitz and his wife Rita Nitz, load the body into the trunk of Michael Miley's car. Boyer stated that Rita drove Michael's car and left, being followed in another vehicle by Richard Nitz. Both Richard and Rita Nitz were arrested for the murder of Mi-chaelMiley.

Rita Nitz   Richard Nitz

During Richard Nitz's trial, he tried to put the blame on a seventeen year old neighbor boy. However, no evidence of this claim was ever found. Richard's defense was, there was no cause of death, since the head of Michael Miley had never been found. A Pathologist at the trial testified that hair had been found in Michael's car, and his death was classified as head trauma. In September 1988, a jury found Richard Nitz guilty of murder, Aggravated Battery, and robbery. Richard Nitz was sentenced to death.

After several appeals, his sentenced was reduced to sixty years. However, the supreme court overturned that, and gave Richard Nitz life without the possibility of parole.

Rita had now gotten divorced from Richard and had remarried. Rita Nitz went to trial in 1989 on the charge of murder. During the trail, Rita stated that Richard had woke her up in the middle of night, stating to her he had gotten his car stuck in a ditch and needed her help. She got up to go help him, and when they got to his car, she said she saw what she thought to be oil on the ground around his car, but it could have possibly been blood. She told the court she didn't know Michael had been murdered.

During the trial of Rita Nitz, it was proven that she had used the credit cards belonging to Michael Miley. Rita's defense in using the credit cards of Miley was that she stated Betty Boyer had given them to her as a gift.

Rita Nitz was found guilty of murder and sentenced to life without the possibility of parole. Michael Miley's head was never found.

CHAPTER 12

MURDER OF CINDY PAVEY

Cindy Pavey

Cindy Pavey, a 22-year-old female, was currently separated from her husband Don, and was living alone in Murphysboro with her two daughters, Tiona age 4, and Misty aged 3. Both daughters had disabilities and required special needs. Cindy loved the two girls very much and was a devoted mother who always took care of her two girls.

On December 2, 1991, Cindy had not been seen or heard of, and a friend went to check on her. When the friend arrived at Cindy's apartment, she found the two small girls watching television. The friend then walked through the apartment, walked to the bedroom door in which was closed, and upon opening the door, she found Cindy lying in there dead, nude from the waist down. She had been severely beaten and was lying in a pool of blood.

Upon autopsy, the pathologist determined Cindy had been dead between eight and twenty hours. Pathologist determined her death to be caused by "blunt force trauma." Cindy had numerous skull fractures in which was the cause of death.

When the Murphysboro Police arrived, they found no forced entry to the apartment. This led them to believe that she apparently knew the killer, and probably let them inside the apartment. There appeared to be nothing taken, nor was anything ransacked in her apartment.

The first suspect police looked at was Cindy's husband, Donald Pavey. The Police had been called several times to their apartment in the past for domestic disputes. Cindy had met with her husband Don a few days prior to her murder pending their divorce.

Another suspect police were looking at was Cindy's boyfriend she had been seeing prior to her death. This boyfriend had had numerous arrests in the past and had been reported as being abusive towards Cindy. The boyfriend walked into the Murphysboro Police Department on his own, willing to talk to them. Police stated he was upset over Cindy's murder, but the Police thought this may be an act he was putting on. The boyfriend stated he had slept with Cindy a couple of days prior to the murder and had been there with her the day of the murder. He stated he left the apartment, and she was still alive.

The boyfriend stated later he tried to call her and could not get her to answer. He stated he thought she was having an affair with someone else. Police checked his phone record and found he indeed had called Cindy several times trying to reach her, but police thought this could be a plot to cover up his involvement in the murder. A search warrant was obtained to get the shoes of the boyfriend to compare them to the footprints at the crime scene. Forensic evidence was checked on the shoes, and nothing was found. The shoes were also the wrong size as those at the crime scene.

Nothing could tie the boyfriend to the crime scene. Now after years, the crime became a cold case.

The two girls Tiona and Misty went to live with their father Don. Tiona was deaf and had been diagnosed with leukemia. Misty had a learning disability and went to live in a children's home in Duquoin, Illinois.

The semen found in Cindy's body at the time of her death, was now sent off for more precise testing. DNA came back to a subject by the name of Quincy Damell Hughes.

Quincy Darnell Hughes

Hughes had an extensive criminal history and was already in the Jackson County Jail on other charges when he was charged with Cindy's murder. Quincy Hughes accepted a plea deal in November of 2008 after admitting to the murder. He received a thirty-year sentence in prison but will probably spend less time. He's expected to be paroled in August 2022.

Tiona Pavey, the oldest daughter, died in 2012 at the age of twenty-five. Cause of death was said to be complications from strep throat because of leukemia.

CHAPTER 13

CREATURE IN MURPHYSBORO

One of the strangest calls I ever received was back in the early 1970's. Murphysboro Police had received a call of a spotting of a large, tall dark "creature," covered in mud by the Big Muddy River. Murphysboro Police had a report from a couple who had been parked at the boat launch at the Big Muddy River. The report was as they were parked, they observed a large creature about 7'0 tall walking on two legs, hairy, and appeared to be covered in mud. Subjects advised it appeared as though the creature was walking towards their car. Sgt. Manwaring of the Murphysboro Police Department stated," the two came to the police department and risked exposing their indiscretions because they were so frightened by what they saw. There was no advantage for them to come up and report this."

Murphysboro Police Department advised the Jackson County Sheriff's Department of this incident. I was working at the time and proceeded to the area to assist in looking for this "creature." We searched the area, but never found anything.

The next evening Manwaring said "he was an officer on duty when a call came in from the Westwood Hills subdivision that two teenagers were sitting on the back porch when they spotted a tall, white-haired, hairy creature in a field just to the edge of the woods."

Sgt. Manwaring contacted Officer Jerry Nellis of the Carbondale Police Department who was a dog handler, and Nellis came over to the area. Manwaring stated that he and Nellis started following a foot path, and Manwaring noticed some slime on the branches, and an odor. The dog tracked the scent to a barn, however, the dog refused to go inside the barn.

Was it the "Big Muddy Monster," that is rumored to be lurking around Murphysboro? Or Was it Big Foot, or Sasquatch? Whatever you want to call it, I guess we will never know. I had heard rumors during my years of law enforcement that the Big Muddy Monster had been seen around Murphysboro since this early 1970's incident, but never gave it a second thought.

Chapter 14

MINNESOTA FATS DOMESTIC

Back in the 1970's Minnesota Fats lived in Dowell, Il, along with his wife and mother n law. We would constantly get domestic calls at their residence. These were always easy domestics to handle. No battery offense, assault offense's, ever took place, just verbal arguments. So, when I or any other Deputy would handle the call, Minnesota Fats would just complain about his wife and mother n law. We wouldn't have to say hardly anything.

He would rant and rave, walk you around his house and show you everything he had materialized, and state his wife still isn't happy. The wife and mother n law would just stand in the back ground, and they never said a word, they would just stand and listen to Fat's talk. After about fifteen minutes of listening to Minnesota Fats carry on, he would calm down, and everything would appear all right.

I remember one night I saw Minnesota Fats on the Johnny Carson show. He was talking about a Cadillac he kept in his yard for cats to live in. Sure enough, he did have a white Cadillac sitting there with cats living in it, for I saw it.

Minnesota Fats was one of a kind. I don't think he would ever raise his hand to anyone. He was actually a nice lovable guy.

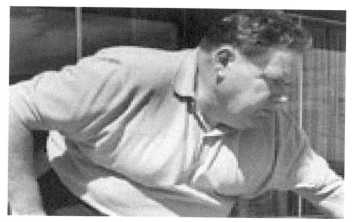
Minnesota Fats

Minnesota Fats, Rudolf Walter Wanderone. He died January 15, 1996.

CHAPTER 15

TROUBLE IN CHURCH

Back in the late 1970's, one of the small towns in Jackson County was having a Sunday night church service. Someone from the church called the Sheriff's Office at the request of the minister, and requested someone come to the church, for they had two male subjects inside creating a disturbance during the church service. The dispatcher advised me via radio, that someone from the church would meet me outside prior to going in.

A short while later I arrived at the church and met with a male subject outside this church. The male subject informed me there was two male subjects sitting on the left side as you walk into the church, about three rolls from the front. He then gave me a description of them, what they were wearing, stating they were seated together. The male subject stated that they had been making loud comments throughout the church service, and the minister wanted them removed.

I then walked in the church while the church service was still going on. The church was full, and all eyes turned on me when I walked in. I walked up to the two subjects, leaned over towards the both of them, and told them I needed to speak to them outside. I was hoping they would comply, and not cause a scene inside the church, especially while church was in service. Fortunately, they complied, and once outside I told them of the complaint, and that they would have to leave. Both subjects complied, and I had no trouble out of either of them.

I never thought I would ever have to go inside a church while church was in service and remove someone. In the profession of law enforcement, you can receive a call of any type, at any time.

CHAPTER 16

BADGE STOLEN

I was on patrol one evening while working the evening shift, and I observed a car sitting on the side of the road on New Illinois Rt #13 between Carbondale and Murphysboro. As I pulled up, I could see the vehicle was occupied by a white female subject.

Upon walking up to the driver's side where the female was seated at, I asked her what the problem was. I saw she had a small child with her. She stated that her car had broken down, for it had just quit running on her. She asked If I could give her a ride home, so her husband could come and get the car. These were the days before cell phones. She stated she would really like to get her child home, and she would tell her husband then. Being the car was a safe distance off the roadway, I never called a tow truck.

I then gave the subject a ride to one of the trailer courts north of Murphysboro where she stated she lived, and I waited for her to get inside her residence before I left. Once she was inside, I then left and went back on patrol.

An hour or so later, it was getting cold out, and I had my police jacket hanging inside the rear passenger door on a coat hanger. I took the jacket off the hanger, put it on, and noticed my badge was gone off the coat. No one had been in my back seat except this particular lady I had given a ride home to, so I knew she took my badge.

I then went back to her residence and ordered her to give my badge back to me. She stated she knew nothing of my badge, and

I told her she took it, no one else had been in my back seat. I informed her if she didn't give me the badge back, I was going to arrest her and take her to jail, and possibly call DCFS for her child. She then walked over to her kitchen table, and picked my badge up and gave it back to me.

Things can happen that you never expect would.

CHAPTER 17

NO GRATITUDE

A Police Officer doesn't expect someone saying "thank You" to him. It's as if no matter what a Police Officer does, the general public thinks that you're just doing your job. We are just doing our job, but it's nice once in a while if someone appreciates what you do.

For example, I was on patrol one Friday evening around 8:00P.M., north of Carbondale approximately a half mile north on US Rt #51. It being a Friday evening, the traffic was extremely heavy. I noticed a lady's purse laying on the highway. Her wallet had come out of the purse and money was on the roadway, and side of the roadway.

I activated my overhead red lights, exited the squad and attempted to retrieve as much of the property as I could. I spent approximately ten minutes out of the squad picking up her items, and picking up as much money as I could find. Traffic did not want to slow down while I was doing this, and it was a dangerous situation. I retrieved approximately $50.00 or more that had come out of her purse, and most of it was change. After retrieving as much as I could find, I then checked the interior of the purse for an ID. I found an Illinois driver's license and an SIU student ID card in the purse. I then advised the dispatcher to try to contact the owner of the purse and tell her I would be bringing the purse to the Office along with its contents.

A few minutes later I arrived at the Sheriff's Office and took the purse into the dispatch room. The dispatcher informed me she contacted the owner of the purse, and the owner stated she would be on her way over to pick it up. The dispatcher stated the owner never even said thank you.

A few hours later, I went to the dispatch room to check to see if the subject showed up for the purse. The dispatcher stated she came about an hour ago, picked the purse up, and never said a word.

At first, it really aggravated me the owner of the purse not even saying thank you after I was out there fighting traffic trying to retrieve her property for her. Then, I got over it, and thought to myself I did my job whether people appreciate it or not.

It is nice if someone says "thank you" for something you did. But we as Police Officers don't expect it, for it very seldom ever happens.

CHAPTER 18

DISRESPECTFUL JUVENILE

One evening I was investigating a Criminal Damage to Property complaint, in which the suspect was a fifteen-year-old male juvenile. I telephoned the parents of the juvenile, and informed the mother that I needed to speak to her son in reference to a case I was working, and asked if she or his father would bring him into the Sheriff's Office for an interview. Mother wasn't too cooperative, however she finally consented to bring her son in.

A couple of hours later, the mother showed up at the Sheriff's Office along with her son, and I took them back to my Office for an interview. When I started asking questions about the case, the fifteen-year-old boy was very belligerent and cursing about every other word. I have never up to this point or after this, ever encountered a juvenile so belligerent towards the Police. The mother just sat there, never telling her son to show respect or for him to shut up, she just let him keep cursing at me.

I told the juvenile and the mother that this interview was over, and if that was my kid, "I would beat his ass for talking to me like that." I then told them to get out of my Office, for I was going for an arrest warrant on the juvenile.

Upon some more investigation of the case, I submitted a report to the State's Attorney's Office, and received a warrant for Criminal Damage to Property o/150 for this juvenile. Upon getting the warrant, I went and served the warrant, and the subject still had the same attitude he previously had with me.

He was found guilty of the charge and got some time in a juvenile facility.

Of all my years in law enforcement, I never encountered a foul mouth, disrespectful juvenile as this one was. And for the mother to just sit and let her son talk this way, no wonder he turned out the way he did.

CHAPTER 19

WILLIAMSON COUNTY TORNADO

On Saturday, May 29, 1982, at approximately 3:05 PM, an F4 Tornado formed NW of Carterville and ripped into Marion, Illinois. During its 17-mile path, it killed 10 people, 181 people were injured, and 1000 people were left homeless. The tornado first touched down about three miles NW of Carterville. It then moved SE through Carterville towards Crainville, then into Marion, Illinois.

I remember it was a nice day outside, and I was out on Crab Orchard Lake, which is in Williamson County, with my dad. We were on his boat working on his boat motor at the time, and we weren't paying any attention to the weather. I remember having clear blue skies when we started working on the motor, and then we became oblivious to the weather due to our attention being on the boat motor. Somewhere around 3:00 PM, I don't remember exactly what time it was, but a boat approached my dad and me and told us we needed to get off the lake due to the tornado. I remember looking up at the sky and how different it was when I last looked at it. It was cloudy, dark, and a very Erie feeling. We then had the subject, who warned us of the weather, tow us into the dock.

My dad and I went back to my parents' house, and once arriving at my parents' house, my mother told me the Sheriff's Office was trying to contact me. She said the Sheriff's Office wanted me to call when I returned. So, I called the Sheriff's Office and was advised the Sheriff was calling everyone into work.

Upon going to work a short time later, I was informed by the dispatcher to go to St. Joseph Hospital in Murphysboro. There I was to pick up an emergency blood supply, transport it to the Marion VA hospital, and transport it code to Marion VA (Code is red lights and siren). I arrived at St. Joseph hospital a few minutes later, and a large supply of blood was loaded into the back seat of my squad car. I then headed towards the Marion VA hospital via Illinois Route #13.

When I got to the area of New Route #13 and the Carterville crossroads, that's when I ran into devastation. Power lines were down in the highway's east/westbound lanes; IDOT was working diligently on these live power lines. The IDOT workers saw and heard me coming and somehow made a path for me to go through. It took me approximately thirty minutes to get to the VA hospital, which is a little less than ten miles from this location.

When I arrived at the Marion VA, numerous people were outside the VA Emergency Room awaiting my arrival. When I pulled up, they started unloading the blood out of my squad.

Once dropping off the blood at the Marion VA, I called via radio and advised the dispatcher that I was "clear." The dispatcher advised that the Sheriff stated to remain in Jackson County, and if Williamson County Sheriff's Office needed us, they would contact us. I then proceeded back to Jackson County.

I still, at times, can see in my mind, to this day, while traveling from Carterville to Marion via Rt #13, the devastation from this tornado. It's something I will never forget what I saw.

CHAPTER 20

ELECTROCUTION

I received a call one evening while working the evening shift of electrocution on Makanda Road east of US Rt#51. The dispatcher advised me via radio that she did not know exactly what had happened except for someone possibly being electrocuted somewhere on the Makanda blacktop.

It had been raining very heavily, and we had strong winds on this particular shift, and my instinct was this would be weather-related. Approximately a mile or so east of Rt #51 on Makanda road, I came upon a tree down on the roadway. A vehicle with its lights on and the motor still running was close to the tree. However, no one was inside the vehicle. I exited the squad and noticed a subject laying on the ground beside the downed tree. Before walking up to the subject, I looked around to check the area and saw the tree was laying across some power lines. It was extremely wet out due to the rain, which at this time had ended. From viewing the subject on the ground, it appeared as though he walked up to check out the downed tree, touched it, and due to the water being on the tree, it conducted electricity form the power lines through the water on the tree to his body. Which meant I could not safely reach him without myself possibly being electrocuted.

I had the dispatcher notify the power company to tell them we had an emergency and for them to get someone here ASAP so I could check on the victim to see if he was still alive. An ambulance was also dispatched to the scene.

When the area was safe, the ambulance crew checked the male subject and found he was deceased. His shirt was partially burned off his back from the electricity, and his back was black from the electricity.

Once clearing the scene, I remember thinking, "why don't people think before they do something." If he had taken a few seconds of thought and visually checked the area, that might have possibly saved this young man's life.

CHAPTER 21

DAY MY SON WAS BORN

One day I will never forget during my law enforcement career was the day my son was born. He was due sometime in the first part of December, and I was working the midnight shift. The night before his birth, we were extremely busy at the Sheriff's Office, and I remember getting off work at 7:00 AM and just wanting to go to bed. But that never worked out.

I found myself at the hospital with my wife in labor, and it was a long labor. I'm not saying that it was several hours of labor because I was tired. Around 3:00 PM, my son was born; what a great feeling!

I thought I would call the Sheriff and, through formality, just request to take this night off since I had no rest. I was a Patrol Sgt then and had to go through the Sheriff to get a day off. I wasn't worried about it, so I called the Sheriff the first chance I got.

I advised the Sheriff my son had been born, and I had worked all night before, been up all day, and was extremely tired. I asked him if it would be ok if I did not come in this next shift. His answer was, "no, I need you to work." No congratulations on the birth of your son or anything. In shock and dismay at his answer, I just stated OK, and I knew better not to say anything else because my temper and lack of sleep would become the best of me. Every time I think of my son being born, this Sheriff comes to my mind, making me come to work that particular shift. In my opinion, that is a complete lack of knowing how to Supervise and take care of your men.

I learned from that and had compassion for my guys if they were ever in a situation where working might jeopardize themselves or others due to their tiredness. We often had to work the midnight shift, be in court most of the next day, and then return to work. Sometimes some of my guys got no rest, so I would let them off and work their shift for them if I was off that night. A good Supervisor ALWAYS takes care of his men...not just because they have your back when working with you, you become like brothers on the road.

CHAPTER 22

UNHAPPY RADIO STATION OWNER

When starting at the Sheriff's Department, one of my first duties was to be a radio dispatcher. The Sheriff wanted each Deputy to know how to work the jail and be a dispatcher before being promoted to the road.

I had put my time into working the jail, and now I was working dispatch. It was customary at the time, at around 6:30 AM, for the local radio stations would call on the telephone to see if you had any news releases to put out. We had had an incident, and I had not been given a news release by the shift Supervisor yet to release. I told this radio station owner I had nothing to put out but should have something shortly after I got the news release. That wasn't good enough for this radio station owner. He started getting irate, wanting to know my name, then started quizzing me on this incident, in which he seemed to have pretty much of what happened, apparently from listening to the scanner previously.

I kept telling him I could not release anything until I received a news release. He responded that he was on his way up to the Sheriff's Office and demanded to talk to me. I informed him he better get here before 7:00 AM, for I was off duty then. I told him he wouldn't demand anything from me, and if I wasn't there when he got here, he could talk to the Sheriff. I then hung up on his ear.

I waited until around 7:05 AM, and no radio owner came in. I wanted to say something to his face, but he never showed up. I then went home, slept peacefully in bed, and returned to work the next night. I heard the subject had come in, talked to the Sheriff, and made a complaint about me, but the Sheriff nor anyone else ever verified that, and I never asked. I didn't care....

Working the radio gives an Officer an insight into what a dispatcher must go through. Their job is not just sitting there taking calls, dispatching them, and dealing with the public. Dispatchers have a lot of things to put up with that we, as road Deputies, don't know unless we had to do the job before working the road. It was a good experience working the radio as a prerequisite to working the road.

CHAPTER 23

CARELESS STUDENT

When being a road Deputy, one must proceed code to a call/location on several occasions due to the nature of the call (Code is red lights and siren).

Carbondale, IL, was one of the worst towns to try to make it through while running code. When a squad came up behind them with red lights and sirens, many motorists would not get out of their way or appeared confused about what to do.

Students walking down the street would see and hear you coming, and some of them would pretend like they were going to run in front of you or pretend they were going to throw something at you. The best thing and only thing one can do is keep on going and ignore their actions.

One night I received a man with a gun call east of Carbondale at the Apartments south of New Rt #13 and just west of Reed Station Road. The dispatcher advised me the subject was currently outside and was threatening to shoot another tenant, and a handgun was drawn.

I was proceeding south on university street in Carbondale and was going to make a left-hand turn onto Walnut street. Approximately one block north of this intersection, a male student was walking, and I saw him turn to look at me. As he looked at me, he stuck his right leg out into my traffic lane, just holding it there, apparently thinking I would swerve to miss him. I kept my speed and stayed in my lane of traffic. If the subject never pulled his leg back, I had my mind made up I would "take it off." At the last second, the subject realized this, and he hurriedly pulled his leg back. As I went by him, I looked in the rearview mirror of the squad at the subject; the subject threw his arms up, looking at me as if to say, "I can't believe you almost took my leg off." I'm sure he never did anything as stupid as that after that.

The general public didn't care if you were trying to hurry to help someone. As long as it wasn't them...

CHAPTER 24

WIFE'S AFFAIR

This call I never handled, for it was handled by another Deputy, Deputy Mosel, at the time. I wanted to include this due to the weird nature of the call.

A Deputy received a call south of Elkville, in which the caller stated that he had thought his wife was having an affair with him whenever he would leave for work. However, on this particular shift, the subject pretended to go to work, then doubled back to look inside his residence without his wife being aware. The subject was alarmed and disturbed upon talking to the Deputy. He stated his wife was having an affair, but it was with a German Shepard dog. The complainant couldn't believe what he saw.

This proves every day in the life of a Policeman is different.

CHAPTER 25

PEGGY'S DISAPPEARANCE

Peggy A. Davis-Johnson Missing since August 9, 1995.

DOB: 06-10-59 Has a scar on the bridge of nose...

Back in the 1990s, I had the opportunity to meet Peggy A. Davis. As far as I can remember, Peggy was never in any kind of trouble, and she just liked to drink. Sometimes, the Sheriff's Office would get a call of an intoxicated female, and I would locate her and take her home. Even though intoxicated at the time, Peggy was always respectful and cooperative with me and other Deputies. Peggy went missing on the evening of August 9, 1995, and her body was never found. Rumors were going around about where her body might be, but nothing ever produced a body from checking the rumors. This is now a cold case, for no one was ever arrested for her disappearance. Hopefully, someone reading this book will see this, and come forward with some information, if they know anything.

On August 9, 1995, Peggy went into a bar in Murphysboro and sat down with two male subjects. After sitting there for a while, the two males stated they were going to Desoto to a friend's house. Peggy allegedly asked if she could go along, and the male subjects consented to her coming along. Peggy allegedly entered a late 1960s Buick and rode with the two subjects to Desoto. Peggy was taken to a friend's house in Desoto, where she continued to drink. The report was she was mixing drinks there and became intoxicated.

The owner of the late 1960s Buick stated he would take Peggy home, for he and his friends were returning to a bar in Murphysboro. The owner of the Buick told Murphysboro Police that Peggy wanted to stop at Hardee's in Murphysboro to get something to eat, so he stated they went through the drive-through at Hardee's. The male subject stated they were sitting on the back lot eating when a female friend came walking up to his car that Peggy knew, and Peggy got out of the car and went with her. The male subject stated that was the last he saw of her.

The next morning, a man was dropping his wife off at work and stated he saw a late 1960s Buick sitting by Hardee's. The man stated a long brown-haired male subject was sitting in the driver's seat, and he appeared to be looking at something with his head down. The male reporting this stated when he came out, the car was gone, and there was a woman's purse laying on the ground where the car had been parked. The police confiscated the purse, which was identified as belonging to Peggy.

The three subjects that had been partying with Peggy the night of August 9, 1995, were all interviewed by the Murphysboro Police. Murphysboro Police Detective Laughland, who was working on the case, stated he didn't believe anything they told him during the interview.

Peggy's body still hasn't been found, and no one has ever been charged in her disappearance/death.

Even though this case is several years old now, hopefully, someone still has information on Peggy's disappearance and will come forward with some information so this case can be closed.

CHAPTER 26

LUCILE FLIGOR HOMICIDE

On November 29, 1978, Lucille Fligor, my fifth-grade teacher's body, was found in her home south of Carbondale. She had been strangled to death. It appears it was a "burglary" of her residence. We don't know if she was home at the time or if she came in during the possible burglary. A German Luger, two semi-automatic weapons, ammunition, and tv were taken from the residence.

Mrs. Fligor's car was also taken during the burglary, a 1975 Oldsmobile. The vehicle was allegedly seen the day of the murder heading towards Carbondale from the south end. The vehicle was found on November 30th in Carbondale. The vehicle was processed for fingerprints, found in the car, and matched up with the ones inside Mrs. Fligor's home. However, no name could be linked to the latent prints, and no one was ever arrested for this homicide.

Mrs. Fligor was an extremely nice lady, and I really liked her as a teacher. It is such a shame someone would do this to her.

CHAPTER 27

RAPE VICTIM INTERVIEW

Deputy John Pavelonis and I worked on a rape case in my early career years. After the victim left the hospital and a rape kit was obtained, Deputy Pavelonis and I took the victim to the Sheriff's Office to interview her. We had no female Deputies at the time, nor did we have any matrons on duty to sit in on the interview.

At this time, the Sheriff's Office was on the south side of the courthouse, and we used the far back east room for an interview room. This was the time the Sheriff lived upstairs in the courthouse.

Deputy Pavelonis and I took the victim to this room and closed the door to do an interview. The victim was upset over the incident, and rightly so. We waited a while for the victim to calm down and get her composure before we started asking questions. After a short while, the victim told us she thought she could talk about the incident now.

Deputy Pavelonis and I chose our words very carefully in interviewing the victim to not upset her more than she was. A few minutes into the interview, the Sheriff came in and, sat down, and started listening to the interview. Again, we were choosing our words carefully, and I reached the point of penetration. The victim still maintained her composure until the Sheriff spoke up. The Sheriff looked at the victim, and right after I asked about penetration, the Sheriff spoke up and asked, "Did he get in your gash?"

The victim then started crying profusely and stated she didn't want to answer any more questions now; she would rather wait and do the interview later. The victim was still crying, and I could not see any reason to proceed with the interview after the Sheriff asked her this absurd question.

We then waited on the victim to call someone to come and get her and stayed with her until her ride arrived. I told her the Detectives would contact her to complete the interview, and she agreed.

This was the most frustrating interview I ever had during my career.

Chapter 28

HOW I GOT THE NICKNAME OF BRUBKR

I like to break away from calls I've been on occasionally and go to a lighter, more humorous side of law enforcement. For example...People always asked me how I came up with the nickname "Brubkr." It came from an incident at work where I was joking around that gave me that name.

I would sit in my Office reviewing reports, doing reports, etc., and would need a break. So, I would pick up the telephone and put it on the intercom where every room in the Sheriff's Office could hear me, even the jail. I would then tap the phone, and in a low disguised voice, I would say, "Hello, Hello; I'd tap the receiver again and say, is this thing working?" I would pause and say, "This here is Brubkr." "You got my boy in jail, and I want him out of there." I would go on for approximately three minutes just talking/adlibbing about my boy being in jail, and I would get irate on the phone about my boy being in jail, then hang up. Of course, Brubkr was fictitious, and I did not have a boy in jail.

After doing this, employees would walk around to different Offices and see if they could figure out who was doing this. They could never figure out it was me, which went on for approximately two or three months. I did it one evening and didn't know the Sheriff was in the building. I thought I was "had" by my prank, but he never said anything; I guess he thought it was funny.

After two or three months of this, one dispatcher returned and caught me on the intercom. The mysterious identity of Brubkr was now out, and the nickname stuck with me. And Brubkr lives on to this day.

I thought it was a good way to keep a little humor in the office and lighten the stress a little for everyone.

CHAPTER 29

OLD CARBONDALE POST OFFICE HAUNTED

Old Post Office in Carbondale, Illinois. Located On West Main and University Avenue in Carbondale, IL.

Over the years, while working, I heard some stories about certain locations in Jackson County, Illinois. These locations are supposed to be allegedly haunted.

I remember going into this post office as a kid with my parents. I remember it had a large lobby when you walked in, and the center of the lobby had a stand with wanted to be posted inside it. I always stood and looked at the wanted posters while one of my parents conducted their business inside.

Rumor goes that the chandelier in the lobby swings for no reason. One night, a janitor working in the building got locked in the closet when no one else was inside the building. There is also a rumor of a lady wearing a long dress that is supposed to float around in the lobby. She allegedly has been in photographs standing behind people who take photos.

Whether these rumors are true or not, I don't know. All I ever heard was rumors.

CHAPTER 30

OLD FRANKLIN COUNTY JAIL HAUNTED

Old Franklin County Jail in Benton, Illinois... closed in 1990

During my early years at the Sheriff's Office, I would sometimes transport or pick up a prisoner at the Franklin County Sheriff's Office. This old jail closed in 1990 and later turned into a museum. It was the same jail where Southern Illinois gangster Charlie Birger was held and later hanged. If you notice, there is a door on the left side of the building. I would use this entryway to deliver or pick up a prisoner.

The jail has since been reported as being haunted. Rumors are that if you record a video in there, you will probably hear voices in the background or a chair scoot across the floor. I read that an individual who was a "ghost hunter" had gone to the cell where Charlie Birger had been held, awaiting his execution by hanging.

The way the inside of the Franklin County Jail looks today.

The "ghost hunter" was inside the cell where Charlie Birger had been held and was taking pictures. The ghost hunter stated he heard someone say, 'You want me to stand over by the screen?' One would assume it was Charlie Birger asking this.

I've heard several stories about this jail since it closed. If you're upstairs in the jail section alone and ask a question, you might hear someone answer you. If you record a video, you might hear voices, screaming, or something one can't describe in the background when you play it back.

When I retired, I took my granddaughter Michele and my girlfriend Angie to visit the Franklin County Jail Museum. There was no set fee for entering the museum, but they wanted you to donate four or five dollars a person to enter. It's basically required you to pay to get in.

Once entering, they want you to watch a video about the jail's history, which is approximately 10-15 minutes long. In the same area, they have a glassed-in case displaying the original noose used to hang Charlie Birger.

Once you watch the video, you are free to wander around on your own. There is no one there who gives you a "guided tour."

I took my granddaughter over to where Charlie Birger had been awaiting his execution and showed her his jail cell. Inside his jail cell, they have a life-like figure standing there of Charlie Birger. While standing there, I made the statement, saying, "Hey Charlie, my name is Shelton." I saw Charlie's figure move when I said that, and my granddaughter said she saw it, too. I believe everything I hear about this jail.

Over the years, I learned that the Choate Mental Health Center in Anna is supposed to be haunted. I transported numerous people there, and I always felt uncomfortable inside that place. Visitors and patients have been reported seeing apparitions, figures, and faces in the windows.

Many people do not know this, but tunnels connect several buildings at Choate, which are reportedly "haunted." One subject ventured into one of the tunnels and swore he felt someone touch him.

It's not just the calls I remember; they're things of this nature.

CHAPTER 31

FROLIC IN A CEMETERY

A strange call I had one evening was when I was driving south on Midland Inn Road and passed the church on the east side of the road. I glanced over at the church when I went by, saw nothing, and proceeded south. While traveling southbound, I had a cable truck pull up behind me, flashing his lights and honking his horn. I then pulled over to see what the subject wanted. The subject advised me he saw two naked people inside the cemetery at the church south of Midland Inn. He stated there was no car he could see, just two naked people inside the cemetery, a male and a female.

I then returned to the location and pulled up to the church's cemetery just north of the church. I radioed the dispatcher, advised them of the call, and exited the vehicle. It was bright daylight then, so it was easy to see around the cemetery. Standing by the squad, I saw no one and walked inside the cemetery area. Behind one of the large headstones was a nude male and a nude female having intercourse. I interrupted their activities and made them get dressed. I ran a wanted check on both subjects, which were not wanted anywhere. After lecturing about not doing what they just did in public, I let them go on their way.

CHAPTER 32

REMOVED PATRONS FROM MIDLAND INN

In the late 1970s, I worked the midnight shift on a Friday night. Midland Inn tavern was in its "hay day" and was going strong. It was an extremely busy Friday night, and we didn't have enough cars on the road to handle all the calls coming in, so some calls had to wait.

I cleared from a call and was sent to Midland Inn Tavern. I was advised by the dispatcher that the bartender had called and stated he had two subjects in the bar causing trouble, and they refused to leave. The bartender had given the names of the subjects to the dispatcher, which I was advised of. I knew these two subjects to be local troublemakers, and they loved to resist arrest. I had no one to assist me on this call, so I had to handle it without backup.

I arrived at Midland Inn Tavern, walked in, and observed the two subjects sitting at the bar drinking. The bartender approached me and stated that these two subjects had been causing trouble in the bar, and he wanted them out. I asked the bartender if they refused to leave; he would sign a complaint, and he said he would.

I then approached the two subjects at the bar and advised them that the management wanted them out of the bar and that they would have to leave or go to jail. The subjects looked at each other, and one of them said to the other, "What ya think, want to go peaceful or not?" They were conversing back and forth with each other, joking about the situation while I was standing there. I told them, "Let's go now, or you're both going to jail." I pulled my nightstick out of my duty belt and told them, "Now, let's go." Both

64

looked at the nightstick I was holding, got up, and left without incident.

One thing about working for a Sheriff's Office or any other Police Department is that sometimes you will have to handle situations by yourself without any backup. You can't let this keep you from doing your job. I had my mind made up; if these two subjects resisted, I might get hurt because they were big boys, but I was putting at least one of them in the hospital with my nightstick. Fortunately, it worked out as it did.

Chapter 33

BARRICADED MAN IN DESOTO

One evening in the 1980s, I was called to assist the Desoto Officer Vince Burns on a subject barricaded in his house on North Hickory Street in Desoto. The subject was holding his wife inside the house; he stated he had a gas can and would set the house on fire. He had been in a domestic dispute with his wife and was very agitated.

When I arrived on the scene, the suspect was inside the house and at the north window. This window was open, and this was how he communicated with Officer Burns, who was by his squad car. The suspect was very agitated and still threatened to burn the house down. I asked him if I could come up to the window and talk to him because I could not hear him very well. After a few minutes, the subject consented for me to approach the house.

I walked up to the window where the subject was talking from the inside and asked him what had led to this. He advised me he and his wife had gotten into an argument and couldn't take it anymore. After talking to the subject for several minutes, I got him calmed down. He told me that he would like to talk to the pastor of his church, and I would call her for him to come to the scene to talk to him. I told him I would have the dispatcher call and advise her.

I had the dispatcher do as I requested, and a few minutes later, the dispatcher called me back, which I answered on my pack radio, still standing next to the window talking to the suspect. The dispatcher advised me that the pastor's husband would not let his wife come to the scene, stating it was too dangerous. Therefore, she was not coming.

Now I'm back to square one with the subject, and the agitation is starting again with him. He now starts to pour gasoline inside his house. Officer Burns and I entered the house and got the wife out safely. We then caught the suspect before he set the house on fire and placed him under arrest.

The actions of this "minister" not helping one of her members could have turned out to be a tragic incident.

CHAPTER 34

SHOOTING AT DENNY'S RESTAURANT IN CAR-BONDALE

Right after I started at the Sheriff's Department in 1972, John Hoffman was still the Sheriff of Jackson County. If I remember correctly, I had been on the road for approximately a year. The dispatcher advised me to meet the Sheriff at Denny's Restaurant in Carbondale, for there had been a shooting there by a Carbondale Police Officer.

Upon meeting the Sheriff at Denny's Restaurant, it was learned that a patron inside the bar had been sitting at one of the tables, had pulled a handgun out, and had just started shooting around the restaurant. Fortunately, he never pointed the gun at anyone and started shooting up high enough not to shoot anyone. The Carbondale Police were called, and one of their Officers had to use lethal force on the suspect because he would not comply by putting the gun down. Since the suspect posed a threat, he had to be terminated.

Since the Carbondale Police were involved in this shooting, the Sheriff's Office was responsible for investigating the incident. At the time, I had to photograph the scene, the body of the deceased, and bullet holes from the suspect inside the Restaurant. Our Detectives were called out to take over the investigation.

It was a righteous shooting, and no charges were filed against the Carbondale Officer. However, the Carbondale Officer quit the Department shortly because he had to kill someone. The shooting couldn't be helped, but the Officers decided whether he could stay in the Department after that and do his job.

For several years after that, I would go into Denny's Restaurant, and I could still see the three bullet holes in the ceiling above the cash register. The bullet holes remained there for years until the Restaurant was remodeled.

CHAPTER 35

DUI CHECKPOINT INCIDENT

Over the years, we worked at several DUI checkpoints throughout the County. We were scheduled for a DUI checkpoint one Friday night on New Route #13, westbound lane at the intersection in front of the Carbondale Walmart. At these checkpoints, driver's licenses are checked, check for DUI, Revoked Driver's license or registration, Illegal transportation of alcohol, etc. Officers from the Illinois State Police, Carbondale Police, SIU Police, and the Jackson County Sheriff's Office were all involved. We would stop as many cars as possible, but if traffic started getting backed up, each officer would stop the fifth vehicle.

I was checking a vehicle with three occupants inside and advised them to pull over to the side of the road. Upon checking the driver's license, it came back that he had a revoked license. I found a valid driver in the vehicle and advised him he would be the one driving when they left. Meantime, I was going to issue the original driver a citation for Driving While License Revoked. Normally, a driving revoked driver is taken into custody and transported to jail, where he must post a $100.00 cash bond. But DUI checkpoints are different; NTA's are issued (notice to appear) for most offenses.

I got in the squad and started writing the citation out, and a Captain with the Illinois State Police came up to my vehicle and told me to hurry up and get back on the line. My being a Sgt., that did not sit too well with me. I then laid the citation book down, exited the squad, and told this Captain I would take as long as I wanted, and if he wanted to push this, I would order him out of the County. The Sheriff is the sole ranking Officer in the County and has the right to order any Illinois State Police Officer or any other agency Officers out of their County if necessary. The State Police cannot tell a Sheriff's Deputy what to do. I told this Captain for him to worry about his own men, and I will take care of mine. He then turned around and walked off. While writing the citation, I lit a cigarette and took my time.

We have always worked well with the State Police, and this is the only time I ever had trouble with one of them trying to order me or one of my Officers around. I needed to take a stand against him, and I did it.

CHAPTER 36

I'M BLAMED FOR SUBJECT'S SUICIDE

One evening, while on patrol, I made a traffic stop south of Carbondale on US Rt #51 for a suspected DUI. Once I got the vehicle pulled over, I found the driver under the influence of alcohol and placed him under arrest.

A tow truck was called to come and get the subject's vehicle, and I then went up to the vehicle to do an inventory for the tow sheet. I found drug paraphernalia in the vehicle at this time. The tow truck arrived and took the driver's vehicle, and I then transported the suspect to the jail for processing. While en route to the jail, I advised the driver that I had found drug paraphernalia in his vehicle and that he would be additionally charged with that. The driver asked me if he could get any jail time for possessing drug paraphernalia, and I told him that would be up to the courts, but it was possible.

About a week later, I came to work and found that my driver, in this case, had committed suicide in some woods south of Carbondale. The charges I had written him were lying next to his body on the ground. A few days later, this subject's parents, uncles, aunts, and his siblings all came to the Sheriff's Office wanting to talk to me.

When I spoke to them, they were verbally hostile and stated that I had killed their son. I tried to explain to them that it was their son's decision I had nothing to do with his death. That made them much more hostile, so I called the Sheriff down from upstairs of the courthouse. When the Sheriff came down, I advised him that the parents and relatives of this subject were here and accusing me of killing their son. I told the Sheriff I tried to talk to them, but they kept becoming more hostile.

The Sheriff then spoke to the subjects, and they became just as verbally hostile with him. Seeing that this would not settle anything, the Sheriff and I then told the subjects to leave the Office, to which they complied. While leaving, they yelled that they would file a suit against me and the Sheriff's Office.

As of this day, I never heard any more from them.

CHAPTER 37

TOBY BURGER HOMICIDE

One evening, I was on patrol and was on the Ava blacktop about two miles off Business Route #13. The dispatcher advised me that a report of shots was being heard around a residence on Melody Lane. I asked the dispatcher if someone was shooting outside or if there was any other information on the call. The dispatcher advised that the caller only said it sounded like it came from a particular house on Melody Lane.

I arrived a few minutes later at the house described, and upon pulling into the driveway, a white male subject came out of the house and walked up to my squad car. I informed him that we had had a report of shots being heard in the area and asked if he knew anything about it. The subject said, "Oh yeah, he's inside; his wife shot him." I asked who was inside and who was the wife. The subject told me it was the Police chief of Murphysboro, Toby Burger, and his wife, Joyce, who shot him. I asked if Joyce was still in the house, and I was advised she was.

I then advised the dispatcher via radio of what I had learned and proceeded into the residence. Upon entering the residence, I observed three handguns lying on an island counter in the kitchen area. A female came running up to me and stated, "Denny, I killed him." I knew the female to be Joyce Burger, for she and her husband Toby were friends of mine.

I found Toby Burger three rooms away, and upon checking him, I found no pulse, and he appeared to be deceased. I then radioed the dispatcher and advised the coroner to come to the scene along with the on-call detectives.

Joyce told me that Toby had found out that she had been seeing the guy who owns this house, the one I spoke with outside, and he was mad about it. She stated she observed Toby drive up outside and park in the driveway, and she thought he was coming to shoot her. Once inside, Joyce emptied one handgun, shot at Toby, went outside, got another gun out of the car, returned inside, and started shooting at him again. Toby tore the curtains off a sliding door, trying to escape the house. However, one of the bullets hit his femur artery, and he died quickly.

When the case went to trial, Joyce was found guilty and sentenced to weekends in the County jail.

CHAPTER 38

INCIDENT AT CARBONDALE HOSPITAL

One evening, I came to work, and the day shift Supervisor told me he had a call that needed to be handled immediately. I said OK, what is it. He stated we had a court order to pick up a 92-year-old woman at Brookside Manor in Carbondale and take her to Carbondale Hospital for a mental evaluation. I was further informed that some family members were with her now at Brookside Manor. I then left the Sheriff's Office and proceeded to Brookside Manor apartments.

Upon arrival, I knocked on the apartment door, and a middle-aged female came to the door. She invited me in and stated she would walk her mother to the squad car for me because her mother would probably put up a fight with me. The subject was placed in the back seat of my squad car. I did not handcuff her because I wouldn't handcuff a 92-year-old lady.

Once I got in the car and started to drive to the hospital, the lady asked me what was going on and where we were going. I informed her of the court order and advised her I had to take her to the Carbondale hospital for a mental evaluation. She became very agitated and started screaming at me.

My squad was equipped with a wire steel screen with holes approximately an inch and a half square. The lady had put her fingers through these holes in the screen, clinched her fingers shut, and yelled and screamed at me to the hospital.

Once at the hospital, I opened the back door to the squad to get the lady out. She refused to comply, kept her fingers clutched to the screen, and would not turn loose. I tried gingerly to get her hands off the screen, but I was afraid I would hurt her, so I stopped my attempt. I then had the dispatcher call the hospital and request some security Officers to come out and give me a hand with her. The dispatcher checked with the hospital and then advised me that the security officers would not help. The dispatcher advised that the hospital security told her she wasn't their problem until she was inside.

I finally got her to turn loose of the screen, and I had to lift her out of the squad car's back seat and carry her inside the hospital. She was screaming and hitting me the whole time. Once inside the hospital, three security officers stood at the door. I put the lady down, and she started tearing everything up she could get hold of and was out of control. Security told me then that I had to take her to one of the ER rooms for evaluation. I told them, "No, you do it. She's your problem. Now she's inside." I then advised the ER staff to call the Sheriff's Office once they determined what they would do with her. I then left the hospital.

Our policy was I was supposed to stay with her until the evaluation was completed. I intentionally broke the policy so the hospital Security staff would have to deal with her. When I left the hospital, all three security officers were trying to get the lady under control and fighting with her.

A few hours later, the hospital called and stated the female needed to be transported to Anna Mental Hospital. The jail staff then transported the lady since the staff made the transports to Anna.

Chapter 39

BREAK AT DENNY'S

When time permitted, and it wasn't busy, sometimes me and another Deputy or two would go to a restaurant in Carbondale and take a break to eat. We would walk in, sit, and order what we wanted. Ninety-five percent of the time, someone would walk up to us while we were waiting on our food and say, "Can I ask you a question?"

Being polite, we would tell them to go ahead and ask. Sometimes, these people would stand there for ten minutes talking to us, even when we were trying to eat. I found that to be very annoying, but being good public servants, we remained courteous to these people.

One Friday evening, another Deputy and I met two Illinois State troopers at Denny's restaurant in Carbondale to take a break. The place was packed; once we got seated, people came in and had to wait for a table. We placed our order, and the waitress walked away. A short while later, one of the troopers sitting with us yelled across the room at the waitress on the other side waiting at a table and told her to come and sit with us. That was very embarrassing, but that was how this particular trooper was. In my opinion, he meant no harm by it; it just wasn't the "cool" thing to do. It was very embarrassing to me.

Another time we took a break, the Desoto Officer Vince Burns told me he would buy breakfast at Denny's for me and two other Deputies. So, all four of us met at Denny's in Carbondale. Once inside, we all ordered, and when it came time for Vince to order, he stated he would just have coffee. I said to him, "I thought you wanted to eat." He stated, "I can't afford it now because you guys are eating." The other Deputies and I never let him forget that incident. We "ribbed" him for years over that.

CHAPTER 40

ARE WE RELATED TO THE SHELTON GANG

Several people asked me, "Are you related to the Shelton Gang? If you are, how did you become a cop?" The Shelton gang was a group of Carl, Bernie, and Earl brothers. They were into so much illegal activity back in the 1920s, stemming from murder, bootlegging, theft, etc. For a while, they were with Southern Illinois gangster Charlie Berger.

The first bomb ever dropped on the United States was when the Shelton gang made a makeshift bomb, flew over Charlie Berger's Hideout between Marion and Harrisburg, and dropped the bomb but missed the hideout. This was after the Shelton gang and Charlie Berger fell out and became bitter enemies. The Shelton's were a feared few in Southern Illinois in the 1920s.

I remember when I was in high school, I visited my grandparents at my Grandpa Shelton's house. We were just sitting around talking, and I asked my grandfather if I could ask him something. I remember we were sitting in the living room, and he was looking outside in his swivel-rocking chair in front of the window. He told me to proceed, and I asked him if we were related to the Shelton gang. My grandfather swiftly turned around in his swivel rocking chair, leaned forward, pointed his finger at me and stated, "Boy, don't ever ask me that again." He then turned around and looked out the window again. So, I dropped the subject. Later, I was in the kitchen with my grandmother, and she told me that when my grandfather would walk down the street, other people walking would get to the other side of the street in case someone drove by and tried to shoot him. My grandmother wouldn't answer my question either since my grandfather wouldn't.

My brothers and sisters and I could never get my father to discuss this. When my father came down with Alzheimer's, he would make a statement now and then about how mean Berny Shelton was. But that's all he would say...

I never did research in Genealogy attempting to trace this down. From my grandfather's reaction to my question, in my mind, he answered my question.

CHAPTER 41

I DON'T LIKE TO FLY

Back when I was in the military, I learned to hate flying. I swore I would never fly again after leaving the military. This was due to my going through an emergency landing on a military plane. However, it seemed as though I had to go every time someone needed to be in an aircraft.

In the mid-1970s, Murphysboro Police Officer Delayne Edwards and I had to fly to Seattle, Washington, to pick up a prisoner. The flight itself was okay, but with my luck, we flew through some bad weather.

The next time I was summoned to be on an aircraft was when Allen Satterfield was the DOT helicopter pilot stationed at Southern Illinois Airport at the time. The Sheriff's Office received a call of four lost hunters around Grand Tower. Satterfield's helicopter was requested to search the scene from the air. A call was made to me to go meet Satterfield at the airport and fly with him to look for the hunters. The weather at this time was terrible. It was raining extremely heavily out, and there were also gusts of wind to contend with.

A short time later, I met Satterfield at the airport, boarded the helicopter, and flew towards Grand Tower. Once reaching Grand Tower, we were told via radio to check the area around the power lines in Grand Tower. I remember Satterfield looking at me and stating, "Keep an eye out for these power lines. I don't know where they're at, and I can't see them." It was raining so hard at this time that we could not even see the helicopter blade turning on top of the aircraft. Approximately five minutes later, we received a radio call that the hunters had been located and that we could clear the area.

We then flew back to the airport, and that was the last time I ever got on an aircraft, and I never will again.

Allen Satterfield was one of the best pilots I ever knew. He had several combat missions in Vietnam, and nothing bothered him while flying. That night, I can say he was nervous. From then on, I absolutely refused to ever board an aircraft again.

CHAPTER 42

WARRANT SERVICE

We had an active warrant on a subject named Henry Ticer, who, at the time, was living at Carbondale Mobile Homes with a female named Teresa Black. Deputy Dave Youngberg and I proceeded to the trailer to attempt the arrest the subject and arrived shortly later.

Upon knocking on the door, the female known to us as Teresa Black came to the door, and we advised her that we were looking for Henry Ticer, for we had an active warrant for him. Teresa Black advised us that Henry was not at home at this time. We then asked if we could look around the trailer to make sure, and she consented to let us search the trailer.

Deputy Youngberg and I knew the subject was in the trailer; we just had to find him. We searched the trailer several times and could not locate him. Out of curiosity, we started opening the cabinets above the kitchen sink, which are not very big. The third cabinet door we opened, we found Henry Ticer all balled up in this little area of the cabinet. We have no idea how he fit into this cabinet, but he did. We ordered him out of the cabinet, and Teresa Black then started getting angry with the Officers for arresting Henry. She then came over and started pushing me and Deputy Youngberg to keep Henry Ticer from being arrested. Deputy Youngberg dealt with Teresa Black while I waited for Ticer to free himself from the cabinet. Once Ticer was out of the cabinet, I placed the handcuffs on him, and he was then advised to walk to the squad car.

Teresa Black was still physically detained by Deputy Youngberg so I could get Henry past her. I told Deputy Youngberg, "Let's take her to jail, too, for obstructing." Youngberg then handcuffed Teresa Black and started walking her to his squad car. I remember looking over to see if he was alright once outside, and Deputy Youngberg had his right arm stretched out to the side, holding Teresa Black by the shirt collar. She attempted to kick him as he walked her to the squad, but she was far enough away that she could not make contact. I couldn't help but laugh; it was one of those things you had to see for it to be funny.

Both were taken to jail and incarcerated. Of course, this was only one of the few times we dealt with these two subjects.

CHAPTER 43

NO "THANK YOU"

It was the end of a long midnight shift, and Deputy Youngberg and I were gassing our squad cars up at the county barn north of Murphysboro. While gassing the squads, we heard a loud crash at the intersection of Rt #127 and Industrial Park Road. We then headed to the location to find out what had occurred.

Upon arrival, we found a one-vehicle accident in which the car was on fire, and the driver was passed out and slumped over the steering wheel. The fire department was called since the fire was too large for our fire extinguishers to put out. We then had to tug and pull the driver to get him out of the burning car. We finally got him out before the flames reached him. Once out, we noticed we knew the subject, a local baker with a drinking problem. The driver also knew us because he made morning deliveries to the Sheriff's Office.

The driver remained passed out once we got him out of the vehicle, and we could smell a very strong odor of an alcoholic beverage coming from him. An ambulance was called, and the subject remained unresponsive even when taken away in the ambulance. His vehicle was a total loss due to the fire it had sustained.

After investigating the accident at the scene, Deputy Youngberg and I proceeded to St. Joseph Hospital in Murphysboro to see if we could speak to the driver. The driver was now conscious upon our arrival, and we were able to speak to him about the accident.

Approximately six months later, I was in the barbershop waiting for my haircut. As I sat down to wait my turn, I could see the subject currently getting a haircut had been our driver in the vehicle fire/accident. I noticed he looked at me when I walked in, but I didn't realize who he was when I glanced at him until I sat down. It was obvious that the subject did not want to make eye contact with me or speak to me. Once he had gotten his haircut, he got up to pay the barber, and he still would not look at me or speak to me. Maybe he was embarrassed or ashamed of us for charging him with DUI; I really don't know.

I thought I would be so grateful to the two Deputies who saved my life; I would have to show my appreciation somehow. At least I know Deputy Youngberg and I did our job, and the subject was alive and well. But, as time passed, it didn't keep the subject from driving under the influence of alcohol.

CHAPTER 44

DEPUTY AND THE CB RADIO

Back in the 1970s and early 1980s, CB radio was a very popular thing. Before we had to take squad cars home, I used to carry a portable CB radio and antenna to work and put it in the fleet squad when I went to work. Several other Deputies did the same thing. We could talk amongst ourselves whenever we wanted and had a good time playing around with them.

We had one Deputy who used the "handle" of "Gravel Gurdy." He liked to talk to the public on the CB and not let them know he was a Deputy. He would pretend he was a citizen driving around and start a conversation with someone. If it was a male subject he would talk to, he would be very polite, and then he would find a chance to insult the subject. The individual he would be talking to would get irate, and they would argue about whatever back and forth on the CB. Some individuals would want to meet with him to "kick his ass," not knowing he was a Deputy.

Other times, he would talk to a female on the CB and carry on a conversation with her for maybe ten minutes or so. After a long conversation with the females he would talk to, he would say, "There's something I've been wanting to ask you. Can I ask you a question?" And the females would always come back and say for him to go ahead and ask. That would be his chance, and he would ask, "You want to meet me somewhere and give me a blow---? You sound so nice." He would tell them what he would do to them sexually. Now the CB radio starts going "nuts." People would get on there and start threatening Gravel Gurdy, wanting to meet him to "kick his ass." He would tell them he would meet them at a certain location and be there in five minutes. He would make up some vehicle he was supposed to be driving and tell everyone to look for that vehicle, for that would be him. I would hear this on the CB, and I would drive by that location ten minutes later, where he told people to meet him, and at times, numerous cars were waiting for him.

Obviously, he never met up with anyone. He was "just having fun." I must admit, it was funny.

CHAPTER 45

ELLEN DRAKE HOMICIDE

On January 16, 1998, Ellen Drake, a schoolteacher who taught at Unity Point School for 27 years, was found stabbed to death in her home on Pleasant Hill Road south of Carbondale by a relative. She was a very well-liked teacher by her students and other faculty members. At the end of the school year, she would write to each student she had, telling them how she enjoyed having them in her class.

The killer tried to clean the residence up free of blood. I was inside the residence, and it appeared to be clean and not appear to be a crime scene as it was. A detective sprayed Luminol on the walls, floors, and all around, and one could see where blood had been cleaned off everything. It was determined that Ellen Drake had been stabbed fourteen times. It was a very gruesome murder. Several items, along with the victim's car, appeared missing from the residence, a new 1998 Toyota.

Witnesses reported that they saw a subject named Gary Dean Lee of Carbondale trying to sell items such as a microwave oven, two TVs, a computer, a stereo, a boom box, a CD player, and a cell phone the night of the murder. Lee apparently returned to Ellen Drake's residence to get more items to sell.

Drake was picked up in Memphis, Tennessee, driving Ellen Drake's new car. Lee had used the cell phone belonging to Drake, and that's how he was located in Memphis. A knife was found inside the car, determined to have Drake's blood on it. The clothes that Lee had also had blood on them, which it was determined belonged to Drake. Lee was transported back to Jackson County and charged with the murder of Ellen Drake and several others.

In court, Lee sold the items taken from Drake's residence to a cocaine dealer. Lee apparently was addicted to cocaine. Lee apparently had done some work for Ellen Drake at her residence. Little did she know Lee would be her demise.

Lee was found guilty of murder and several other charges and was given a life sentence.

CHAPTER 46

AMANDA BOLIN HOMOCIDE

Amanda Bolin Age: 14

On September 22, 2002, Amanda Bolin, age 14, of Murphysboro, was picked up at Murphysboro High School by subject Shane Harvey, age 20, from Desoto, Illinois. Harvey was allegedly going to take Bolen to a friend, but she never showed up. The mother then later reported Amanda missing.

A hunter called the Jackson County Sheriff's Office two months later and stated he saw a human skull while exiting a field approximately a mile and a half east of Murphysboro near Route #149. The skeletal remains were found approximately forty feet away from the skull. The skull was determined to be human. Sheriff Kilquist surmised that there were many animals in the area, which could be why the skull was separated from the rest of the remains. Dental records revealed that it was the body of Amanda Bolin.

The Sheriff's Detectives interviewed Shane Harvey, and Harvey told police another individual killed Bolen. The detectives interviewed the other man, and he denied killing Bolen. This subject stated that Harvey dropped him off at his father's house in Elkville on September 20th, and Harvey then drove away with Bolin.

During an interview on November 5th, Harvey told police that he accidentally killed Bolen while wrestling when he dropped her. In the November 6th interview with Harvey, he told police that Bolin kicked him in the scrotum while they were wrestling. Harvey stated he lost control and then strangled Bolen.

On November 5th, Harvey was arrested in Desoto, Illinois, on two counts of first-degree murder and concealment of a homicidal death of Bolen. He was found guilty in a court in Jackson County. Harvey was sentenced to twenty-six years in prison by Judge David Watt.

CHAPTER 47

ARREST OF ANOTHER POLICE OFFICER

In the late 1970s, and even some today, the small towns in Jackson County hired their own Police Officers to work their town. When they were working, this helped our department out tremendously, cutting down on our workload, etc. However, a lot of these towns did not do a background check on their Officers when they hired them.

I came to work one night and was advised by the evening supervisor that he just discovered an outstanding warrant for "bigamy" out of Tennessee on the Dowell Officer. Tennessee requested that we arrest the subject because they wanted to extradite him.

This particular night, this Officer was on duty in Dowel. I told the dispatcher to call him on the radio and tell him I needed to speak with him at the Sheriff's Office. The dispatcher complied, and a short while later, the Dowell Officer arrived at the Sheriff's Office.

Our Office at this time was in the SE portion of the Courthouse. When he came into the Office, I told him to come back to the back office, for I wanted to talk to him. We went into the back office, and the first thing I did was to advise him I needed to see his duty weapon. He handed it to me, and I told him that Tennessee had contacted our department and advised us that they had a warrant for him for bigamy. He didn't seem surprised, and I then advised him he was under arrest on said warrant.

I then took him to the jail's booking area, where he was then incarcerated on said warrant. The city of Dowell was called, and they sent someone later to pick up their squad car. The suspect was still in a Police uniform when I arrested him, and I was not proud I had to do this. It put a sinking feeling in me to arrest another Officer.

Tennessee came and got the subject a few days later, and that was the last I saw of this Officer.

CHAPTER 48

MY SQUAD HIT TWICE

Of all the miles the Police Officer drove, I was fortunate to be involved in only two accidents. Both were not my fault.

I was on Patrol one evening. It was around 10:00 P.M. I was at the red light at Rt #127 and Route #149, facing west. This pickup truck was northbound on Rt#127, and when he reached the intersection I was at, he slammed on his brakes and tried to turn right on Rt #149. He hit my squad car head-on instead of turning into his lane. Our vehicles were stuck together from the accident, and he made several attempts to back up to free his vehicle from mine. He broke loose, backed up, and headed east on Rt #149. However, when he got even with me, he made the mistake of stopping and then looked over at me. I exited my squad, ran to the driver, and pulled him out of the truck. The subject was highly intoxicated, placed under arrest and taken to jail. My squad had several thousand dollars' worth of damage done to it.

I was on Business Rt #13 in the second accident, just north of the railroad bridge. I was sitting in the southbound lane with the overhead red lights on, on the squad car, due to a bad accident at the railroad Trussell on Business Rt #13. I was detouring traffic on Harrison Road, and we were not allowing any traffic around the accident site. A southbound vehicle was coming at a high rate of speed, and I had the traffic cone on my flashlight, trying to get him to stop. The subject never even hit his brakes; he ran into the back of my squad, doing major damage to it. This subject, too, was highly intoxicated. He was arrested and charged with DUI and several other charges. He was taken to the Jackson County jail after I had to have my squad towed and another unit to come and take my place to stop traffic.

Of all the miles I have driven while on duty, I was fortunate to have only these two accidents on my record. It aggravated me because both were not my fault.

CHAPTER 49

RIDE ALONG

One evening, while working, I had one of our dispatchers with me who wanted to ride along. The policy was that if you were employed at the Sheriff's Office, you could ride along with a Deputy if the Deputy consented.

Deputy Youngberg and I then received a call to go to Carbondale Mobile Homes about a violent domestic. Deputy Youngberg and I arrived at the same time out of coincidence. As we pulled up to the trailer, a black male came running out the trailer's door, followed by another black male. The second black male had a gun in his hand, stood in the trailer doorway, and started shooting at the subject who had just run out of the trailer. I told the dispatcher riding along to grab the shotgun in case I needed it and stay behind me.

Deputy Youngberg and I exited the squads, and the suspect with the gun saw us and took off running to escape. We searched the area and found the suspect a few minutes later, hiding under another trailer. We apprehended the subject, and he was placed under arrest. We learned the suspect had come home and found another male subject in the trailer with his wife, the subject the suspect had shot at.

I looked around for my rider, and Deputy Youngberg nor I could see him anywhere. When I returned to the squad car, I saw him sitting in the passenger seat, and the shotgun was still in the rack. He told me he was scared and never got out of the car. He then asked me to take him back to the Sheriff's Office so he could go home.

That was fine; he was not a sworn Deputy, and I understand his fear. He never asked to ride with anyone again after riding with me.

CHAPTER 50

VIOLENT DOMESTIC

One evening, I was on regular patrol, and Deputy Youngberg and I sat north of Carbondale just talking. We then received a call of a violent domestic at Carbondale Mobile Homes. The report was the caller stated they could hear a female inside the trailer screaming.

We located the trailer and walked up to the door. Upon arriving at the door, we could hear a female inside screaming and yelling. We knocked on the door and yelled, "Sheriff's Dept." However, no one came to the door. The screaming continued, and we tried the door and found it unlocked. We entered the trailer and found a black male subject on top of a female, beating her with his fists. We ordered him to stop and, at the same time, ran up to the suspect, and we had to pull him off the female.

The suspect started resisting, and he seemed to be extremely strong. Deputy Youngberg and I fought with him for at least ten minutes, trying to put the handcuffs on him. We later learned he was on PCP. I thought I was in shape then, but I could hardly walk the suspect to the squad after we subdued him; I was so tired. As Deputy Youngberg and I are "Old School Cops," we take them to the ER, not the morgue.

The female subject signed a complaint against the suspect, and he was taken to jail after leaving the hospital.

CHAPTER 51

"BUDDY BUDDY" HARRIS

When I first started at the Sheriff's Office, I was advised by the Chief Deputy at the time, Woodrow Procunier, that if an arrest warrant ever came down for subject Buddy Buddy Harris, to call him on the phone, tell him there's a warrant, and he will come in and take care of it. Woodrow advised me that Buddy Buddy drove a white pickup truck, and when driving, he would always have one of his men following him. I asked why he was any different than anyone else warrants came down for, and Woodrow just advised me to comply with his request.

I later learned that Ed Lavern "Buddy Buddy" Harris and his Lieutenants controlled all the vending machines and jukeboxes in Jackson, Union, Williamson, Alexander, and Pulaski Counties.

An investigation commission sent two undercover agents down here regarding Buddy Buddy Harris. The two agents pretended to want to set up a vending machine route in this area. They met with Harris at his saddle club west of Murphysboro, and Harris told them at this time, they had been marked for murder as a result of trying to start their business down here in this area. Harris told them to return to Chicago, never come back trying to set their business up here, or they would be killed, just like two other competitors, Howard Baker and Burnice Tyner. These two were murdered on July 27, 1968, and January 28, 1960.

The two agents then drove off in a rented car they were driving, and they were ambushed by a man hiding in some bushes down the road. The subject in the bushes riddled their car with bullets. They then ran off the road but escaped uninjured.

Harris and his associate George Garner were indicted on October 28th, 1968, by a Union County Grand Jury on numerous charges, with no charge of any murder. He got out of the charges because he was still around when I started at the Sheriff's Office in October 1972. He was the owner of the Hilltop Tavern west of Murphysboro. The bar later burned down, and he never had it rebuilt.

On February 10th, 1970, three men tried to kill Harris at his bar west of Murphysboro. He had three shotgun blasts go off at him and was hit with the pellets, but he survived his injuries. The barmaid at the time was taken hostage. Harris's saddled club was also destroyed by fire. After this, the vending machine wars subsided. It was speculated that Harris got scared of the attempt on his life and went into early retirement. He spends most of his time now on his property around Kinkaid Lake.

Sometime in 1973, we had a warrant come to our office for "Buddy Buddy," I don't remember what the warrant was for now. However, I called Buddy on the phone and informed him of the warrant and the bond. He thanked me for calling and said he would be in in a few minutes to take care of it.

I waited at the Sheriff's Office, and in about thirty minutes, Buddy showed up to take care of the warrant. He was courteous to me, posted the bond on the warrant, and then left. That was the last I ever heard or seen of him.

CHAPTER 52

STOPPING ANOTHER POLICE OFFICER

Over the years, I have stopped so many vehicles for traffic violations that it's impossible to say how many I have stopped. I've had many people ask me, Have you ever written another Police Officer a citation for anything." I was one who always tried to show Professional Courtesy when stopping another Officer, i.e., I did not want to write another police officer a traffic ticket. But to answer the question, yes, I have written another Officer.

I was on New US Rt #51 south of Carbondale on Friday evening, running emphasis patrol. Emphasis patrol is where you concentrate on a certain highway or a section of that highway to enforce traffic laws. I had moving radar in my squad, and I would drive south on Rt #51 to Makanda road, turn around, and drive north maybe five miles or so, looking for speeders. It's easier to catch speeders like this rather than sitting on the side of the road clocking them.

This Friday evening, I was heading North on New Rt #51, approximately four miles north of Makanda Road. I had a Corvette approaching me, and I clocked him doing 92mph in a 55 mph zone. I turned around and stopped the subject, and upon stopping him, I learned that he was an FBI agent. The subject advised me he had been working on his car and was trying it out. I never asked to see his driver's license or his insurance card. I told him to slow it down because there was too much traffic on this road to drive that fast. He was polite, apologized, and stated he would slow down. I then let him go.

Exactly one week later, on a Friday evening, in almost the same spot, I stopped the same FBI agent again for doing 93 mph in a 55-mph zone in the same Corvette. I stopped him and got him pulled over just north of Makanda Road. When I walked up to the driver's vehicle, I stood behind the driver's door a little so he could not see me. I asked to see his driver's license and insurance card and if he knew why he was being pulled over. The driver said he did; he had been driving fast to try his car out, for he had been working on it. I then moved up to where he could see me. I told d him I had stopped him exactly one week ago for going 92 mph, and I let him go.

He rolled his head when I told him, looking as though to say I'm caught. This Friday, he gave me the same excuse for speeding, so I told him I was writing him a citation for speeding 93/55 mph zone. The driver was polite and never tried to argue with me. He was cited and let go. I followed him south on New Rt #51 for several miles before I turned around. Obviously, he had not been working on his car, for he continued to travel south, not turning around to return home. I'm sure he did the same thing the prior week.

I can honestly say that's the only other Police Officer I ever wrote a traffic citation to, and I never felt bad about it. Police Officers are like brothers and take care of one another. But this Officer knew he had it coming.

Another time I was on New Rt #51 south of Carbondale running emphasis patrol, I stopped a northbound unit going 83 in a 55-mph zone. I then turned around and pulled the vehicle over. As I got up to the driver's side door to speak with the driver, who was female, I heard a male subject in the back seat say to me, "Write her, Shelton. I've been telling her all night to slow down." I looked in the back seat and noticed it was Judge Watt, a judge in my County; his wife was driving. Another female was seated in the front seat, and another male was in the back seat with Judge Watt.

I told the driver and Judge Watt I wouldn't cite her. I told Judge Watt I was leaving it up to him to make her abide by the law. Judge Watt and I conversed briefly, and then I let them drive on.

Many people would say you play favorites out there enforcing the law. No, we don't play favorites; it's called professional courtesy. We make mistakes like everyone else. I've let many citizens off in the past with a verbal warning for a violation, much more than I have Police Officers and judges. I call it compassion, common sense, and caring for each other.

CHAPTER 53

WORKING THE DUQUOIN FAIR

Back in the early 1980s, the Duquoin Fairgrounds was privately owned. At this time, the owners of the Fair would request any Officer interested in working during the Duquoin Fair to put their name on a sign-up sheet. Deputy Jim Nesler of the Jackson County Sheriff's Office was responsible for this.

Deputy Brent Mosel and I signed up to work at the Fair, but we told Deputy Nesler we wouldn't work anywhere except the grandstand. Deputy Nesler consented, and Deputy Mosel and I worked several nights at the fair.

Several shows went on without incident. Deputy Mosel and I would work the gate on the south side of the stage that went back to the dressing rooms. Basically, our job was not to let anyone through the gate without a pass. We worked the Red Skelton show, Tammy Wynett show, the Gatlin Brothers show, and Kenny Rogers show, just to mention a few. I got to meet some of these stars. Red Skelton was extremely nice.

Just before Red Skelton went on stage, he was informed that his house in California was burning, and it didn't appear it would be saved. Skelton was allowed to leave and not fill his contract due to the fire, but he refused. Red Skelton stated he could do nothing and had a show to put on. When he was on stage, one would never know he had his house on his mind. He gave a great performance that night.

One evening, Willie Nelson had a show at the Grandstand, and Deputy Mosel and I were assigned to work that. Instead of working the gate by the stage, we were told to patrol the fences and area around the grandstand to keep people from trying to sneak in. Deputy Mosel and I walked over to the north side of the grandstand to check this area, and we observed probably thirty people or more climbing the fence, attempting to get in to see the show. We tried to prevent this, but this was virtually impossible. We gave up, and we were fighting a losing battle. We let them do it if they wanted to climb the fence to get in, which was probably twenty feet high.

During Willie's show, the crowd was getting very rowdy. Officers working the grandstand were told to stand before the stage to prevent anyone from getting on the stage. There were approximately thirty of us Officers lined up in front of the stage. We were holding people back trying to get on the stage.

I was pretty much in front of center stage in front of Willie. He started signing Whiskey River and threw his hat in the crowd during the song. The crowd started getting wilder and rowdier when he did this. Holding people back from trying to get on the stage was hard. I heard Willie say something, and I turned around and asked him what he said. He told me, "Let 'em go." He then stopped singing and headed for his bus. Officers then walked away from the front of the stage after he left. The crowd pretty well calmed down when they saw Willie leave the stage.

During one of the other shows Deputy Mosel and I worked on, the head usher was supposedly a schoolteacher. This man thought he was our boss and tried to tell us what to do. After ignoring his requests several times, he started getting arrogant towards me. I then informed him he wasn't my boss and to keep clear of me; I might just arrest him for obstructing if he kept hindering me. Of course, I wasn't going to arrest him, and I told him this to get him to back off. He quit trying to tell us what to do but would make sarcastic remarks towards Deputy Mosel and me. If I wasn't a Police Officer, I'm afraid of what I might have done to this teacher after the show. That's how bad his attitude was.

After this particular year at the fair, Deputy Mosel and I were done working on it.

CHAPTER 54

BRAKE FOR DEER

One evening, I was sent to a domestic call south of Carbondale. Upon arrival, I learned that the husband had beaten his wife, and she had several lacerations and bumps on her face. The husband was arrested for domestic battery, handcuffed, and placed in the back seat of my squad car. After the ambulance left to transport the wife/victim, I proceeded to the jail's booking area.

While en route to the jail, the suspect scooted up behind me and yelled through the steel-caged screen. He was right in my ear and would not be quiet. He was calling me names for arresting him and being extremely irate.

The suspect's face was about a foot from the steel caged screen between the front and back seats. After a few more minutes of him yelling and not listening to me tell him to be quiet, I slammed the brakes as hard as possible. The subject's face smashed against the steel screen, busted his nose, bleeding, and a few other cuts. I then radioed the dispatcher and advised that I had to brake because a deer ran out before me, and the prisoner in the back seat hit his face on the steel screen. I further advised that I would stop by the ER before booking.

The suspect was treated at the Emergency Room at St.Joseph Hospital, and I then transported him to the jail. The suspect never said a word from the hospital to the jail.

CHAPTER 55

MURDER OF PAUL RAINS

Loy Eugene Hines was a tavern owner in Murphysboro, Illinois 1973. For some reason, he strongly disliked the subject Paul Rains, age 29, of Murphysboro. That dislike drove Hines to the point where he orchestrated the murder of Paul Rains.

Hines confronted Rudy Dean Weberling, age 26, a former Murphysboro resident, on June 26th, 1973, to kill Paul Rains. Weberling refused to take the offer. Hines then solicited Charles Robinson of Dupo, Illinois, to kill Rains. Hines paid Robinson $2000.00 after Rains was slain for doing the job.

A former St. Louis police officer, John Earl Bauchens Jr., age 33, was present when the contract was made between Hines and Robinson to kill Rains. Bauchens later purchased overall-type clothing at a St. Louis store for Robinson and another unknown man to wear when killing Rains. Rains was abducted from his trailer outside Murphysboro and taken to a wooded area. At the wooded area, Rains was then killed with a shotgun blast. Hines and Robinson were later found guilty of murder by a Jackson County Jury. I never did learn who the other man was with Robinson at the time of the murder.

After the trial, I and another Deputy were assigned to take subject John Earl Bauchens, the former St. Louis police Officer, back to the St. Louis County jail. We were instructed not to converse with Bauchens or ask him any questions.

About halfway to St. Louis, I told the other deputy that I was hungry and asked if he wished to stop to eat somewhere. Bauchens, shackled in the back seat of my squad car, stated he was hungry too and would like to stop. We pulled into a steak house; I exited the squad, opened the back door, and handcuffed Bauchens to the steel cage in my car. Bauchens stated he wished to go in with us to eat, and I told him, "Not today, son." I told him I'd bring him a hamburger. The other deputy and I went inside and enjoyed a steak dinner while keeping an eye on Bauchens in my squad. Once we finished eating, I took Bauchens a hamburger out, and I made sure the hamburger was cold, uncuffed him from the steel screen and, handed him the hamburger and told him to "enjoy."

We then transported Bauchens to the St. Louis County jail and proceeded back to Jackson County.

CHAPTER 56

IGNORANCE WILL GET YOU ARRESTED

One morning, I was home mowing my yard for my day off. A motorcycle pulled up in front of my house, stopped and started revving the engine. I looked to see who it was, and it was a subject I knew by the name of Smokey Jones. I knew Jones currently had a revoked driver's license. I ignored him, and he kept driving in front of my house for about ten minutes, revving his engine.

The next day, I went back to work, and I wrote a report on the incident and sent it to the State's Attorney's Office requesting a warrant for subject Jones. I came to work a few days later and saw the Smokey Jones warrant lying on my desk for Driving While License Revoked. I then proceeded to Jones's residence, located him at home, and arrested him on the warrant. He couldn't believe he was being arrested for this offense. I told him, "Jones, I know your driver's license is revoked. You shouldn't ever mess with me at home."

Jones pleaded not guilty to the charge, and the case went to court. Jones brought his brother with him, and the brother got up on the stand and stated he had been the one who had been driving the motorcycle in front of my house. Judge Watt, the presiding Judge, took a recess and stated he wanted to see me and the State's Attorney in his office.

Once in the Judge's chamber, Judge Watt asked what was happening. I told him the brother was lying, for I had a clear view of Smokey Jones that day driving the motorcycle, and he was by himself on the bike. Judge Watt stated, "Good enough," he then turned to the State's Attorney and asked him if he wanted to go for a per-jury charge against the brother. The State's Attorney stated he wouldn't pursue it, and the court was reconvened.

Smokey Jones was found guilty of the charge and sentenced to six months in the county jail by Judge Watt. He was now in jail over Christmas and was in jail the day his son was born. He paid the price for his ignorance.

CHAPTER 57

IMPERSONATING A POLICE OFFICER

One evening, I was driving through Carbondale, and I had my girlfriend with me. I was westbound on Main Street approaching Poplar Street and driving in the far-left hand lane. Out of nowhere, this pick-up truck pulled up to the right side of my truck, and the driver had his window down, cursing and making threats towards me for no reason. I asked him what his problem was, and he kept calling me names, threatening to "kick my ass." My girlfriend then showed the subject my Police ID and told him to back off. He yelled, "—ck You, everybody has one of those."

He then told me to follow him and pull over, to which I complied. I took his actions as a disrespect for the badge, so I followed him to the old Ramada Inn in Carbondale. On the east side of the Ramada Inn were some large trailers, and he pulled in between the trailers.

I got out of my truck, showed him my Police ID, and asked him what his problem was. He stated, "I have one of those, too." I asked him if he was a cop, and he stated he was a Williamson County deputy. I told him to show me his Police ID, and he said he didn't have it. He then started calling me names, and I informed him he better back off or he was going to jail. He got in his truck, drove, and parked in front of the Ramada Inn. I drove by his truck, obtained the registration number, and called the Sheriff's Office. I asked the dispatcher to see if the registered owner was a Williamson County Deputy, and after a few minutes, the dispatcher advised me Williamson County Sheriff's Department stated he was not. I then had the dispatcher send a Carbondale Police unit to my location.

Once Carbondale Police arrived, I signed a complaint against the subject for impersonating a police officer. The Carbondale Police Officer then located the suspect inside the Ramada Inn, and he was arrested and later transported to the Jackson County Jail.

Once at the jail, my girlfriend's stepfather was one of the jailers on duty when the suspect was brought in. Her stepfather told the suspect when he came in, "This isn't your day, you –ck with an off-duty cop, and I'm his girlfriend's stepdad, you're screwed."

I thought justice was served that day, even without going to court.

CHAPTER 58

STORIES OF THE GRAND TOWER

What Used to Be the Grand Tower Bank Located at Front Street and Market Street

My father grew up in Grand Tower, Illinois, and was telling me one day about the old bank in Grand Tower on Front Street at the corner of Market Street. He stated years ago, possibly in the 1930s, there was a hold-up at the bank, and a shootout ensued during the robbery. He told me if you look on the corner of the building, you can see where bullets ricocheted off the concrete during the shootout. I stopped by there in the 1970s one day while working to see if I could see the ricochet imprints. I found them, but they were starting to fade/wear off the building. But they were there.

My late uncle, Oscar Wills, worked at the Grand Tower Power plant for 30 years. On March 22nd, 1973, he was working at the Power Plant when and received a phone call from a co-worker. The co-worker asked Oscar if he would go outside and look above the transformer bank and for him to see if he could see anything above it. Oscar stated he went outside, and above the transformer bank was an object shaped like a donut with high-intensity lights. He told me the lights were red and white and spun around the donut-shaped object. The object appeared to have windows, but the windows remained stationary.

Oscar said it hovered around maybe 20 minutes, and then it took off. He stated there was no motor sound or nothing coming from the object; it was completely silent and flew right over him when it left. Oscar stated about 25-30 minutes later, three or four jets made eight to ten sweeps around the power plant, apparently looking for the object. My uncle stated he never reported the incident to the Police. I told him he should have called the Sheriff's Office, but my uncle wasn't one to report things of this nature.

Tower Rock in Grand Tower, Illinois

There have been numerous stories of Tower Rock, Devils Bake Oven in Grand Tower, about it being haunted. One story was that there was a drowned wedding party that resurfaced and said there was going to be a civil war before the civil war.

At one time, there was a house on top of Tower Rock where a wealthy man lived with his beautiful daughter, Esmerelda. The father was reported as being very protective of his daughter and did not want her to see anyone. She met a riverboat captain that her father did not approve of and forbade her to see him again and locked her away in the house. One report was the riverboat captain died, and Esmeralda could not handle this. Esmerelda left her room, and her body was found on the river bank the next morning. It's been reported that when the moon illuminates Tower Rock, a mist can be seen going through the trees, and when the mist is gone, one can hear the moaning of a woman.

Whether this story is true or not, I don't know.

CHAPTER 59

VIOLENT DOMESTIC

The dispatcher called me one evening and advised me of a violent domestic on North 20th Street, the last house on the left. The dispatcher further advised that it was a violent domestic; the husband beat the wife.

I arrived a short time later, and upon walking up to the house, I could hear some screaming from a female. As I got to the house's front door, a small boy around six years old, maybe a little older, was at the front door. He cried and advised me, "My daddy is killing my mommy."

As I looked inside the residence, I could see a female on her back on the kitchen floor and a male subject on top of her, beating her with his fists. I then entered the residence, grabbed the male subject, and pulled him off the female. The male subject then got into a karate stance and threatened me. I then attempted to subdue him, and I was able to get him on the floor, and I was attempting to put handcuffs on him.

While fighting the subject and trying to handcuff him, someone behind me said, "Oh no, you don't." I looked over my shoulder, and the female victim, the suspect's wife, had a 32oz glass Coke bottle and was just getting ready to hit me in the head with it. Sgt. Manwarring of the Murphysboro Police Department had just arrived to assist me on the call, and he had grabbed the female victim and taken the glass bottle from her. He struggled with the female, and both subjects were subdued and arrested.

The small boy who met me at the door had an aunt nearby. She was then called to come and take care of the boy. Several years later, I learned that the suspect I arrested had become a minister in a church.

CHAPTER 60

EMBARRASSMENT IN COURT

One of the most embarrassing moments I have ever had in my life was the time I was called to go to court in Randolph County.

It was back in the mid-1970s. I was married at the time and living in Desoto. I was out mowing my yard, and it was an extremely hot day. My wife said I was supposed to call the State's Attorney in Randolph County ASAP. I then got off the mower, went in, and called.

Upon speaking to the State's Attorney, he advised they had a jury trial going on at that moment and needed me to come up and testify. The man on trial was one I had previously arrested before his getting arrested in Randolph County. The State's Attorney stated that the jury was in the jury box and was waiting for me. He further stated I was exempt from all laws traveling to Chester courthouse and to get there as soon as I possibly could.

I told him I never got a subpoena for the trial, and the state's Attorney stated he knew that this just came up. I told him I needed to shower first, and he stated not to come the way I was and to get there in a hurry. Before my arrival, I told him to explain to the jury why I looked like I did. He stated that he would, and I'm hoping that he did.

I got in my car and headed to Randolph County Court House. Now, I had extremely dirty clothes on, I had been sweating for the last two hours, and my hair was wet from sweat, in addition to "hat hair." I was a mess...

I arrived, walked into the courtroom, and was greeted by the State's Attorney at the door. The courtroom was almost packed, and the jury looked at me like I had been living on the street. I could not believe this was happening to me. I always wore a suit, if not my uniform, to court because I was meticulous about my appearance. From the looks I got from the jury and the spectators in the courtroom, I could easily interpret what they were thinking.

I was on the stand for approximately fifteen minutes, which was the longest fifteen minutes I have ever had. If I had to repeat it, I would make them wait while I cleaned up before leaving.

That was the most embarrassing moment I have ever had in my life.

CHAPTER 61

SHOPLIFTERS IN THE DAY

When I started at the Sheriff's Department in 1972, this was before any Wal-Marts or K-Marts were ever around. We had the Grandpa Johns store north of Murphysboro, the Grandma store just west of Grandpa Johns, Cousin Fred's in Carbondale, and Sav Mart east of Carbondale. Sav Mart was located on the southeast corner of New Rt #13 and Reed Station Road. Sav Mart later moved out, and the store then became a Tipton's store.

During this time, there were no shoplifter detectors one had to walk through when exiting the store that would go off if an item had not been paid for. There were no bar codes, and the prices of items were on a small paper sticker stuck to the item. The stores would hire security people who watched for shoplifters, and they would pose as regular customers. I.E., customers did not know there were people there watching for shoplifters or taking a price tag off the item and putting a cheaper price tag on it. As I said, the prices were merely put on an item with a small paper sticker, and they were easy to remove and replace with another cheaper sticker.

On each shift, we would inevitably get at least one call, if not more, to Grandpa John's or Sav Mart east of Carbondale for shoplifters. When I received a shoplifter complaint, I would arrive at the store and find that the management and security would have the suspect/s in an office waiting on me. I would be informed of the occurrence and then ask if the store wished to press charges, which they always did.

One would think that shoplifters would be people with little money or juveniles doing the offense. But to my surprise, 90% of the time, well-to-do citizens committed the offense. I've even arrested Professors at SIU for shoplifting. Many times, people would say they just wanted to see if they could get away with it. I thought that was a huge gamble and severe consequences to satisfy one's curiosity.

These stores started to close, with Wal-Mart and K-Marts moving in. It was an era in my past in which I did not have to deal with shoplifters.

CHAPTER 62

SEARCHING BAR PATRONS

Jackson County used to have many bars. We had Carrie's Tavern, Midland Inn, Road Runner Club (later the Dumoroc), JB's Tavern, Wards Tavern, Bird Cage, plus the bars in Dowell. These were the ones on the east side of the county.

On the west side, we had the VFW, Red Buoy, the White Rose, and a few more bars downtown Grand Tower. We had Polly's Bar and Grill, Kinkaid Tavern, and the Chinch Bug on the county's west side. We also had all the bars in Ava and Campbell Hill we had to deal with. Especially during the weekends, most of our calls were bad calls.

Carries bar, which was also Kilo's and other names during my tenure, was located on Old Rt #13 just east of the Big Muddy Bridge. The black community mainly patronized this bar. We had numerous fight calls in which people would get hurt and reports of shots being fired. We would have people shot in the parking lot and, at times, people being the victim of a knife wound in the parking lot.

After several months of these calls at Carrie's bar, I went to talk with the Sheriff. I told him I would like to get some Officers from Murphysboro P.D., SIU Officers, State Police Officers, and possibly some Carbondale Officers to search the patrons inside the bar for guns. The Sheriff advised me that he thought that would be a good idea and that I should set it up.

I had numerous Officers from other departments, and we met at the Sheriff's Department and proceeded to Carries Bar. Once at the bar, I had two officers standing at each door, preventing people from leaving, and the rest of the patrons were lined up against the wall. The patrons were searched for weapons, and numerous guns were confiscated from individuals. In addition, we made several arrests on warrants we learned were active on some of the patrons.

This quietened the bar for a few months, and then it went back to how it was: fights, shootings, stabbings, etc. Maybe we prevented someone from getting killed those months after our "raid" while it was quiet.

CHAPTER 63

EARLY DAYS OF DRIVE-IN

In the 1970s, we were fortunate enough to have Drive-In Movie theatres in the area. Waring Auto Theatre on Old Rt #13 was between Murphysboro and Carbondale, which later changed its name to Campus Drive-In. The Waring Auto Theatre opened on July 3rd, 1948, accommodating. On July 19, 1967, its name was changed to Campus Drive-In when it was sold to a new owner. Unfortunately, it closed September 18th, 1977, and was demolished. That was the beginning of the era that ended Drive-In movie theatres.

These drive-ins were always busy and crowded on the weekend. As one entered Campus Drive-in, there was a winding drive when you turned off Old Rt #13 leading up to the ticket booth. The drive was windy to keep the traffic from backing up on Old Rt #13. At times, patrons lined up all the way to Old Rt #13 in line, waiting to pay to get into the drive-in.

I used to enter the drive-in occasionally while working. I would pull up to the ticket office, talk to the ticket agent inside the booth, and check if everything was going alright. After talking to the ticket agent, I would drive into the theater and patrol up and down the lanes between the cars. When driving in the drive-in theater, it was understood that headlights were turned off, and one would drive with parking lights on only.

I used to patrol this area to let people know we were watching for underage drinking, fights, etc. Many moviegoers would bring lawn chairs outside their vehicles, but most would sit inside their cars. Although always quiet and peaceful, I still patrolled to let people know we were around.

This is just a little reminiscent of the early days of my career. I enjoyed the drive-in theaters so much that I hated to see them die off. It seems like all the good things in life never last. It's a shame that young people today can't enjoy what my age group used to enjoy.

CHAPTER 64

DIRTY COP

After I retired, I was retired for a few years and got bored doing nothing. I saw in the paper the Southern Illinois Airport Police had an opening for a Police Officer. I then applied for that position and got the job.

To work for the airport police, one has to have all his police schooling completed, and you have to have experience working as a Police Officer, i.e, when I started working for the airport police, all Officers were tenured. We had officers working there with other departments as far away as Chicago. In all, they were a good group of guys.

After working there for a couple of years, one of the officers invited me and my girlfriend to his house for dinner. We accepted the invitation and had a good time. When we left, my girlfriend said she had something to tell me, and I wouldn't like it. I asked her what it was, and she proceeded to tell me.

She stated the Officer's wife took her into the bedroom and opened a dresser drawer by the bed. Inside the drawer was some marijuana and other controlled substances in there. This was before the time that marijuana was legalized. She further stated that her husband makes a trip up north once a month and brings back some controlled substances and marijuana. The wife further informed my girlfriend that she stated she had marijuana mailed to her at the Marion, Illinois, post office. It's addressed to her but in her sister's name.

I went to work and got in contact with the police chief at the time and informed him of the incident. I requested that each officer be called, and we had a random urine test done for drugs. He agreed and got it ok'd through the airport manager. When this officer was called to go immediately to the hospital with the rest of the officers, he refused and stated he could not make it. This happened several times when he stated he could not make it. The chief told me the airport manager wasn't going to push it. I then contacted the Sheriff, met him for coffee, and informed him of what was happening. He stated he would rather I contact the DEA and gave me an agent's name to call.

I called the DEA agent and gave him the information about the Marion Post Office, where the officer's wife was receiving marijuana through the mail. I gave the agent the officer's vehicle information and the registration number and told him about this officer making a monthly trip to pick up marijuana and possibly controlled substances. The DEA agent didn't seem to be concerned, and it appeared to me from talking with him that he didn't want to be bothered with this incident. I couldn't believe it, but after thinking about it, it didn't surprise me DEA was this way.

I then waited a few weeks to see if DEA would do anything about this, and they did not. I then contacted a friend on the airport board and informed him of this Officer and what he was doing. I told the board member that DEA wouldn't do anything, and I did not want to work with someone of this caliber. The board member then went to the airport manager, and the Officer was let go.

I have never been one to be a "whistleblower," but when it comes to an officer doing something illegal, you bet I will report it. All the other officers working at the airport the fifteen years I was there were all good Officers, and as far as I know, have never done anything illegal. If one is a police officer, then he/she should live his/her life like one and obey all the laws. People watch everything we do.

I have never felt bad about this officer losing his job, and I would do the same thing all over again.

CHAPTER 65

TRANSPORT OF MONEY

In the 1970s and early 1980s, Murphysboro had a bank called The City National Bank. It was a very good bank at the time, for that was where I did my business. I hated to see it close.

One day, I went to work, and Woodrow Procunier, the Chief Deputy at the time, called me into the back office and stated he had a job for me. He informed me to go to the City National Bank in Murphysboro and meet with a subject there who was a bank employee, for they needed money transferred to the University Bank in Carbondale. The University Bank was located on West Main Street in Carbondale and has since closed.

As requested, I went to the bank and contacted the subject I was supposed to contact. He then said he would load the money in my squad car to go to the University Bank. The employee and I walked the money to the squad, a large white bag about the size of an army duffle bag. I asked him how much money was in the bag, and he told me $225,000.00. The bank employee put the bag in my back seat, closed the car door, and started to walk back into the bank. I never signed anything stating I received the money. I stopped the bank employee and asked him where he was going, and he stated he had to get back to work inside the bank.

I told him, "Oh no, I'm not being left alone with this money, for I don't know how much is in there except for what you told me." I further informed him that he would go with me to the University Bank to transport the money, and I would bring him back. He stated he would then but needed to go to the bank and tell them. I told him no, he was staying with me and the money, and I would have my dispatcher call the City National Bank and tell them he was making the transport with me.

The bank employee went with me to the University Bank, where he and I took the money inside the bank. I then gave the City National Bank employee a ride back to the bank. No way was I going to transport this money by myself, especially only on the word of the bank employee of how much money was in there. If it was short of the amount he said it was, then I know who would have been to blame for the missing money. Me...

CHAPTER 66

CARBONDALE HALLOWEEN

One of the things I used to dread the most was the time during the Carbondale Halloween party on South Illinois Avenue in Carbondale. This party went on annually during the 1970s but cut back a little in 1988.

All the Deputies were issued riot helmets, and we were told to keep them in our squad cars and ensure we had them during Carbondale Halloween. These parties consisted of drunken brawls, riots, and sexual assaults during this time, to mention a few incidents. The comedian John Candy made a film in 1980 of the Carbondale Halloween party for an NBC show called "Road Show." The Carbondale Halloween party was known throughout the United States.

Thousands of people and SIU students would flock to Carbondale to party on South Illinois Av. The Sheriff's Department was to remain outside the city limits of Carbondale during the party and be ready to assist the Carbondale Police if they needed additional help. South Illinois Av was blocked off around Grand Street in Carbondale, and northbound traffic had to detour around.

Some partygoers would get into groups, walk around Carbondale and start vandalizing things. Cars were turned over, beer was thrown at people, and numerous crimes were committed, along with broken store windows. In 1988, Carbondale attempted to cut back the partygoers by banning alcohol the week before Halloween. This meant no alcohol could be sold in Carbondale the week before the party, and bars would stay closed. Students were then sent home for a mandatory five-day break.

The South Illinois Halloween party dwindled a bit during this time, but students who lived off campus held parties during Halloween. Groups of people would still walk through Carbondale, turning cars over and breaking store windows.

In 2000, the city of Carbondale decided to open the bars and stop liquor sales restrictions before the Halloween party. The Halloween party of 2000 was back, almost a riot. Store windows being broken out, cars being overturned, vandalism everywhere. When I retired from the Sheriff's Office, I was glad I didn't have to mess with the Carbondale Halloween party. Every officer there during the party should have received "combat pay," I believe it was that bad.

Milton Keynes UK
Ingram Content Group UK Ltd.
UKHW020244251123
433118UK00011B/132